Stars in the Window

A True Story of Homelife During WWII
–
The War on the Home Front

By

Jean Bradford Kline

authorHOUSE™

1663 Liberty Drive, Suite 200
Bloomington, Indiana 47403
(800) 839-8640
www.AuthorHouse.com

First published by AuthorHouse 01/04/06

ISBN: 1-4208-9091-3 (sc)
ISBN: 1-4208-9090-5 (dj)

Printed in the United States of America
Bloomington, Indiana

This book is printed on acid-free paper.

Table of Contents

Bradford Family

Only photo of the Bradford family. Mother, Clara, (see shadow) taking picture of happy-go-lucky Bradford kids taking sister Jean for a wild wagon ride. Dad Bradford in background chopping wood.

Alden, Winona, Junior, Jean, Lyle & Kyle

Bill & John holding their pet calf "charcoal."

Youngest of the nine children born after the first picture was taken

Index of Pictures & Illustrations

Dedication

This book is dedicated to my paternal grandmother, mother, father, brothers and sister who this story is all about.

Of the nine original children there are five left: Winona, Kyle, Jean, Bill and John. Lyle was tragically killed in a plane accident in 1951 at the age of 23, and Geneva died at six months. Junior and Alden passed away leaving wives, children and grandchildren. Now there are over 50 members of the Bradford family who gather once a year at Christmas time in Eaton Rapids. This book is also dedicated to them with the hope they will appreciate their heritage and pass it along to present and future generations.

This book is especially dedicated to my brothers, Junior, Alden, Lyle and Kyle, who represent the four stars in the window which are the subject of this book. Also, to my brother-in-law, Bob Davis, who married my sister and then immediately went to serve his country.

Four Stars in the Window:

Walter M. Bradford, Jr., U.S. Army; Alden J. Bradford, U.S. Navy;

Kyle & Lyle Bradford, U.S. Navy.

Bob Davis, U.S. Army Air Force, Winona Bradford's husband

Acknowledgments

A BIG thank you goes to:

My sister, Winona, who read every word and wore out her red pen making corrections.

My friend, Marie Lotta, a published author, who read the final text and offered her constructive suggestions.

My husband, a WWII veteran Pacific Theatre, who made suggestions and "pushed" and "prodded" me to continue on. Without his support this book would never have been written.

To Howard Umbarger who shared his experiences as a prisoner-of-war of the German Government. He told of his horrendous experience and of being liberated by the Russians on February 3, 1945. He and other prisoners found their own way home by mostly walking to Naples, Italy where they boarded the U.S.S. Wakefield and set sail for Boston Harbor, U.S.A. Howard finally arrived home to Eaton Rapids on April 29th, almost three months after his liberation.

And finally a Thank You goes to all of you who have contributed personal information and waited patiently for this publication.

Preface

Many books, dozens of movies and thousands of articles and reports have been written about WWII. Several books have even attempted to picture what happened on the home front to ordinary citizens in cities, small towns and rural America.

Unpretentious, patriotic and hardworking American families sacrificed, supported and contributed to the war effort. *Life* and *Look* magazines, and various photographers used photographs to catch special moments and report developing news in weekly and daily newspapers across the nation. Today's senior citizens remember certain images on government posters used to sell war bonds, promote the war effort and protect the vital US arsenal of materials, war supplies and weapons.

Michigan was known as the "Arsenal for Democracy" and the center of the American effort to provide guns, ammunitions, jeeps, trucks, naval vessels, liberty ships, bombers, transports and fighter aircraft to battle Hitler's legions and the Japanese war machines. Even today's school children have probably seen war posters like "Rosie the Riveter." "Uncle Sam Wants You," and "Loose Lips Sink Ships," among others. But very few have read or been told the "real story" of the war effort on the home front. How school children and adults skimped and saved, collected and recycled, made do and did without. They shut off lights at night, participated in air-raid drills, built bomb shelters, saved pennies, bought war bonds, collected fat and milkweed pods, and followed a rigid and restricted rationing system to limit the purchase and use of all critical materials essential to wartime production.

Unlike today's conflicts in Iraq, Kosovo and Afghanistan where the mainstream media focuses on the tragedy of a few deaths a day, the drama and terror of thousands of dead in a single battle or naval engagement is no comparison to the hype and media hysteria of present conflicts.

This true story is written to preserve the valor, unflinching effort and uncomplaining sacrifices made at home to support our fighting forces. There are a few books that touch on the home front but none, that I know of, really tell the day-to-day life struggle and efforts of an ordinary family that has sent its young men off to war with the knowledge that many of them will not return. While there are always a few people who will shirk their duty, flee to another nation or claim to be conscientious objectors, you will not find them in this true account of small town America. With a population of less than

5000, it is interesting to learn that over 640 men and women served in WWII in one of the armed forces.

I hope you will enjoy reliving this important era in our nations history where boys quickly became men and girls and women became overnight male replacements for the sons, husbands, brothers, and fathers represented by blue stars in a front window of a majority of homes in almost any community.

This story is about a family who sent four sons off to war. Did any of the blue stars turn to gold? You will have to read on to find out more about the almost forgotten saga of War on the Home Front that affected the lives, fears and dreams of every person in America during the great worldwide war from 1942 to 1946.

Introduction

As a grandmother now and a young girl then, I can't think of a more turbulent time during my life than the years of WWII. It began for the United States in the Pacific on December 7, 1941 when the Japanese conducted a sneak attack on our navy ships anchored in Pearl Harbor and the protecting airfields. At the same time, Germany was defiantly attacking and sinking our merchant ships in the Atlantic.

In the beginning, we were nearly defeated by the combined forces of evil on multiple fronts. The only thing that was not beaten was the indomitable spirit of the American people on the home front and the courage and valor of our fighting forces in far-flung battlefields and oceans.

Everyone pulled together. Young men and women volunteered for service both at home and abroad. The factories were quickly converted to produce tanks, airplanes, jeeps, trucks, ships, uniforms, guns and ammunition, instead of cars, farm machinery and household appliances, civilian goods and apparel.

Women put on flannel shirts and men's work pants, and with their hair wrapped in bandannas, filled many of the new jobs in the factory, as well as those the men left behind. Nylon stockings were no longer available, so women working in offices painted their legs to look like nylons complete with an eyebrow pencil line up the back to resemble the seam.

Every household was asked to save cooking fat, newspapers, scrap metal, tin cans, string and any piece of rubber, and at the same time urged to raise their own food. The school children bought ten-cent war stamps, picked milkweed pods and acted as guinea pigs to test special nutritional food for the service men. You may remember the K-rations and later the improved C-rations that were fed to our men on the battlefields.

Gasoline was scarce and rationed, food, sugar and coffee were rationed, new automobiles were no longer made, and car parts and new farm machinery were unavailable. War time, or fast time as some called it, was introduced to save on electricity in the factories and to give folks more daylight time to work on their victory gardens and farmers to work in their fields. Of course, without lights farmers worked from dawn to dusk and by moonlight regardless of what time the clock said.

The home front fought the war valiantly and furiously while they sent their young men and women into the jungles and islands of the Pacific, the deserts of North Africa and on to the shores of France and into Germany.

It took four years to beat them in their attempt to conquer free nations but the U.S. finally prevailed. We pushed Hitler's best troops back and brought Germany to her knees. Then we stopped Japan's warlords and took back the Philippines. Just about every house displayed a flag with a blue star for each person serving in the war. At the Bradford household, my home, four blue stars graced the window and hence, the name of this book.

The United States sent 16,353,659 men and women into the various armed forces, Army, Navy, Marines, Air Force, Coast Guards, Merchant Marines, and Sea Bees. Battle deaths claimed 292,131 lives. Deaths from other causes claimed 115,187. The wounded numbered 671,801. Captured or missing numbered 139,709. The United States asked only for space to bury their dead. A bronze plaque at a U.S. Cemetery in France records these words: "When you go home tell them of us and say for your tomorrow we gave our today."

You can only imagine the impact these numbers made on this country and its citizenry. Unfortunately, gold stars replaced many blue stars for those who tragically gave everything to preserve the freedoms and sovereignty of our nation. Yes, this was the greatest generation who served willingly without rancor or bitterness.

Great sacrifice was also made on the home front. This book is a true story of a single family in small town America and their struggle during the war years. It is about their sacrifice, their ability to do without and their devotion to each other and to their country. Other stories have been written about WWII but this book focuses on the home front during those years and the war's impact on every family in the United States.

WWII poster to encourage enlisting

Chapter 1

The First Blue Star

Clara unrolled the small flag and looked for a tack to secure the nine-by-eleven-inch silk flag in the front window. With its patriotic red border and a single blue star in the middle of a white background, it announced to those who drove by that from this household a member was serving in the military service of the United States.

She wasn't the only mother hanging a flag in her window, many others were, too. Ever since that dreadful attack on Pearl Harbor nearly a year ago on December 7, 1941 and the declaration of war that followed, Clara feared for this day. She feared for the day her tall, handsome and robust twenty-year-old son would be drafted into the service.

"But I want to go, Mom!" he told her. "Alden can take over my farm chores and the twins are getting big enough to help more on the farm. . . And besides, it's the patriotic thing to do!"

She knew he was right and the "greetings" he held in his hands said he must go. But how could the family ever get along without him? He was her firstborn. Walter, Jr., named after his Dad and called Junior only at home, and Walt by the outside world, the one who brought fun and laughter to the house, who looked after the younger children, who worked in the fields and the one who always complimented her on her good cooking. “Boy, that was good, Ma,” he would say after almost every meal, his broad smile exposing his perfect white teeth. She couldn’t bear the thoughts of losing him, or any of her other seven children for that matter.

Before looping the gold-braided rope over the tack, she spread a solution of vinegar and water over the window glass. Crumbling up a page from yesterday’s newspaper she rubbed the glass until it squeaked clean. It sparkled in the western sun. She wanted to make sure all passersby would notice the single blue star beaming out from the front window of the dilapidated old farmhouse which sat along a dusty dirt road in rural Michigan.

“I’ll write as soon as I can,” he had told them at the train depot. “And thanks, Dad, for the wristwatch, it’s the best!” With a handshake and a hug he had boarded the train and was gone, leaving his parents on the platform waving until the train disappeared from sight.

Before leaving the window, Clara stepped back to view the flag to make sure it was hanging straight. Bending her head slightly to the right and then left, she adjusted the flag accordingly.

A view from the road was necessary before the task could be declared complete. Leaving the house, the slight-framed woman passed into the sunshine of the early fall day. She hardly noticed the rickety porch with loose and broken boards. The dormant spirea and lilac bush on either side of the steps flexed their bare limbs to her passing. The air was fresh. The gentle breeze played with her graying hair as she continued down the drive and onto the road to see for herself just how the motorists would view the single star in her window.

Somehow this particular blue star was so very meaningful. She had seen blue stars in other people's windows, some had as many as two or three. She knew what it meant, but this star- - this single blue star meant her very soul had gone to war. She couldn't put her thoughts into words if asked. Nor could she explain the feeling she had as she stood on the side of the road scrutinizing the window in her own home. She wanted to cry, but pride dwarfed her feelings of sadness. She wondered if other mothers felt this way.

She waved to the neighbor lady across the road and pointed to the window. She returned the wave and smiled her approval. Clara felt fortunate to have neighbors so close by. She had jokingly told folks that the Bradfords now lived in Swanville. Of the four families on this stretch of road, three of them were Swans. It was a comfort to know that all of them were merely a brisk walk away. The Swan family across the road had a phone, a rarity in this neighborhood, and were very willing to let the Bradford family use it in case of an emergency.

Knowing the other children would soon be home from school, she must go in and start supper. The big red, white and blue school bus would soon pull up in front and the children would be home. They would spill out of the bus and run to the house like a herd of young colts. She hoped they would notice the star in the window.

Walking back to the house she wondered what lay ahead for her family. How long would this awful war last? She remembered that the last war, only twenty years ago, was "the war to end all wars." What happened? Would Junior come home safely when it is over? Would any of her other children be called to serve?

We highly resolve that these dead shall not have died in vain.

Remember December 7th!

Chapter 2

The Family at War - - A typical Farm Day

Each day Clara scoured the day-old State Journal searching for news of the war. Unlike the city dwellers where the daily paper is delivered by paper boy on the day it is printed, the paper was delivered by the rural mail carrier for subscribers in the county. Therefore, the paper was always a day old when it arrived in the mailbox by the road.

Every evening she sat in front of the radio listening to Edward R. Murrow or H.V. Kaltenborn broadcast the evening news. No one dared to talk to her from seven to seven-thirty while the accounts of the war were described in vivid detail.

The first phase of the war in the Pacific was disastrous for the Allies. After Pearl Harbor, Japan swiftly conquered the Philippines, Malaysia, Burma, Indonesia, and many Pacific islands, and destroyed an Allied fleet in the Java Sea. They reached their farthest points of advance in the Aleutian Islands west of Alaska and in New Guinea just north of Australia.

The first Allied naval successes against Japan were scored in the battles of Coral Sea and Midway. On land the Allies took the offensive on New Guinea and landed on Guadalcanal in the Solomon Islands.

In spite of the small accomplishments, it was perhaps the darkest period of the war for the Allies. In the Atlantic, even to the shores of the United States and in the Gulf of Mexico, German submarines were sinking Allied ships at an unprecedented rate. Yet, the Axis war machine started showing signs of wear, while the United States was just beginning to put its potential into motion.

Clara agonized over all the boys who had lost their lives. Each one was someone's son. She wondered how many mothers would be exchanging the blue star in their window for a gold one. She felt relieved that her son was safe and not one of them. She affectionately patted her apron pocket which held the most recent letter from Junior.

"When I finish basic training I'll come home for a 14-day furlough before being shipped out," he wrote. Clara wondered where he would be shipped to. She knew he couldn't tell her even if he knew. If he did, it would surely be cut from his letter when it went through the censors' searching eyes. All letters from the service men were censored before being sent on their way. Any information which could be used by the enemy was simply cut from the pages, regardless of how insignificant it might seem.

"He will be home for Christmas!" she said out loud. That was the most important issue right now. She could hardly wait to see him. How handsome he must look in his uniform. She must fix his favorite food and invite his friends in, those who hadn't already been called into the service.

But, after his furlough, where would he be shipped? Would it be where the fighting is so intense? How much danger would he be in, she wondered. She must put those nagging thoughts aside and focus only on his homecoming and being home for Christmas. That was the primary event right now. Well, that and putting the final touches on tonight's supper.

Supper preparations were going well. Grandma Bradford was at the kitchen range browning flour, wet with bacon drippings, in the big black skillet. Her specialty was making "poor man's gravy," the final dish for supper tonight. Ten-year-old Jean had placed the right number of chairs around the table. She counted a total of nine plates. It was only a short few months ago there were eleven. Junior's plate had been removed when he was drafted, and later Winona's when she married and moved to Battle Creek.

It hurts a mother so to remove plates from the table. Nevertheless, the remaining six children filled the house with noise and laughter. Alden quit high school at seventeen and took over Junior's farm work. The identical twins, Lyle and Kyle, only two years younger, worked on the farm while attending high school; the younger boys, Bill, age six, and John, age four, made up the Bradford Boys. Jean was the only girl at home. She was in constant conflict with the older boys, either hating them intensely or loving them totally all in the same hour.

At the supper table, Clara announced "Junior will be home for Christmas. He will finish his basic training and have fourteen days at home."

"Wow, Mom, do you think we will know him?"

"Oh, of course we will! He will be in uniform and his hair will be cut really short, but we will know him," she assured the young ones. Junior being gone a few weeks seemed like ages to a child.

"Will he bring his gun home?" another asked

"Will he show us how to kill Hitler?"

"Ya, Mom, will he show us how to kill a Jap?"

"Do you think he still knows how to milk cows?

"I bet he forgot!"

"No he hasn't, dummy. No one forgets how to milk a cow," another mocked.

"He can't work in the barn 'cause I 'm wearing his boots!" Alden chimed in.

"We must fix his favorite food," Grandma added. The supper table was usually full of talk and lots of laughter, just like Clara's large family when she was a child. Interruptions were made occasionally by Clara trying to instill good manners in her children. "Don't talk with your mouth full!" "Get your elbows off the table," and "Don't talk so loud," were her usual commandments.

Now everyone was talking at once. They really weren't expecting answers nor responses, they were just excited that their big brother was coming home.

The kitchen was warm from the heat of the cookstove and the aroma of supper wafted through the big kitchen. Boiled potatoes, with poor-man's gravy, baked beans and fresh homemade bread covered with yellow butter was the standard supper. Meat, which was strictly rationed, was reserved for Sunday dinner only. A quart jar of cherries was opened and divided equally into individual sauce dishes for dessert.

Outside darkness was falling, bringing with it an added chill.

"Come, boys. Finish your supper, we got milkin' to do." Dad, a man of few words, spoke from the head of the table.

Before supper while the cows were in the barnyard, one boy pumped fiercely while they drank from the watering tank. The other boys cleaned the stanchions, put in fresh straw and filled the manger with hay from the loft above, before the cattle were let in. After supper all that was left to do was the milking.

Dad was typically the first to leave the supper table. His actions were always the same and somewhat mechanical as he rummaged around in the pocket of his patched overalls for a match. He struck it against the black iron cookstove. It lit with a pop and from it he lit the barn lantern and then his own pipe from the same match. He reached for his shapeless old gray felt hat from its nail by the door, and placed it securely on his head. All that was left was to put on his knee-high rubber boots before he was ready for the barn.

It usually took extra prodding from Mom to get Alden and the twins moving toward the barn and the after-supper chores. It was obvious that none of the boys shared their father's love for the land.

There was, however, no prodding tonight. They were eager to get the chores finished and get back into the house to write Junior a letter. He was coming home!

From the stack of clean, shiny milk pails turned upside down on the reservoir of the kitchen stove, they each took one. The twins placed theirs over their heads like a helmet and goose-stepped, Nazi style toward the barn, while Alden called out the military cadence with a feeble attempt to use a German accent.

"Those boys! What one can't think of the other will!" Clara shook her head and laughed.

After Grandma and Clara finished the dishes and the dishpans were put away, Clara went back to yesterday's Journal, wanting to make sure not one scrap of war news was left unread. She handed Grandma each section of the paper as soon as she was finished.

Grandma read the news and kept up on the events of the war and of the political news of the day. She could talk politics with the best of them, and did at every opportunity. She held an opposite view from Harry, her son-in-law, and when she visited her daughter, Eva's home, she was instructed not to discuss politics. Fortunately, Walter held his mother's political view.

The younger children could hardly wait for Grandma to finish reading the news. They knew as soon as she was finished, she would turn to the children's story and read it aloud. Each day there was a new story in the paper just for the young ones.

She thumbed through the paper biding time for the twins and Alden to come in from the barn after the evening chores. Even though they were now older, they still enjoyed the evening ritual of Grandma reading to them from the daily paper. She had read to them since they were babies. The youngest sat on her lap while the others sat on the floor hugging their knees at her feet. Alden, viewing himself as being too old for children's stories, pretended not to be listening from across the room.

She folded the paper to the proper section, cleared her throat, adjusted her glasses, and commenced to read.

For a half hour the children were whisked away to a land of make believe where there was no war or want, where the children were always happy, and where good overcame evil. They visited faraway lands they never heard of, were introduced to children who were different than they but were exposed to difficult situations that someday they might face.

For the time being the Bradford household was in harmony.

UNITED STATES OF AMERICA
OFFICE OF PRICE ADMINISTRATION

535991 AJ

WAR RATION BOOK No. 3

Void if altered

NOT VALID WITHOUT STAMP

Identification of person to whom issued: PRINT IN FULL

Larry J. Holley

(First name) (Middle name) (Last name)

Street number or rural route ....

City or post office .... State ....

AGE	SEX	WEIGHT Lbs.	HEIGHT Ft. In.	OCCUPATION

SIGNATURE ....
(Person to whom book is issued. If such person is unable to sign because of age or incapacity, another may sign in his behalf.)

WARNING

This book is the property of the United States Government. It is unlawful to sell it to any other person, or to use it or permit anyone else to use it, except to obtain rationed goods in accordance with regulations of the Office of Price Administration. Any person who finds a lost War Ration Book must return it to the War Price and Rationing Board which issued it. Persons who violate rationing regulations are subject to $10,000 fine or imprisonment, or both.

OPA Form No. R-130

LOCAL BOARD ACTION

Issued by .... (Local board number) (Date)

Street address ....

City .... State ....

.... (Signature of issuing officer)

PROCESSED FOODS

Green stamps K, L and M good through March 20. Blue stamps A8, B8, C8, D8, and E8 valid through May 20.

MEATS, CHEESE AND FATS

Brown stamps Y and Z valid through March 20. Red A8, B8, C8, D8, E8 and F8 valid through May 20.

SUGAR

Stamp 30 in Book 4 good for 5 pounds indefinitely. Stamp 31 in Book 4 good for 5 pounds starting April 1. Stamp 40 in Book 4 good for 5 pounds for canning through Feb. 28, 1945.

SHOES

Stamp 18 in Book 1 valid through April 30. No. 1 airplane stamp in Book 3 good until further notice.

GASOLINE

A-10 good through March 21. A-11 valid March 22 through June 21. B-1 and C-1 stamps good for 2 gallons until used. B-2, B-3 and C-2 and C-3 good for 5 gallons.

TIRES

Next inspections due: A book vehicles by March 31; B's by June 30; C's by May 31; commercial vehicles every 6 months or every 5,000 miles, whichever is first.

FUEL OIL

Periods 4 and 5 coupons valid through Sept. 30; all have value of 10 gallons for each unit. All change-making coupons and reserve coupons good throughout heating year.

Ration Book that was issued to each individual. Schedule of coupons to use for each rationed item, found in most newspapers

Chapter 3

Rite of Ration Books

"Boys, I want you to gather up the walnuts in the yard and put them in the driveway. We've got to get the husks off and let them dry a spell before we crack them." Clara was talking to the three older boys. After trying almost every other method to shuck the disagreeable husks, it was a proven experiment that placing them in the drive and letting the vehicles run over them was the best way to loosen and remove the stubborn husks. Preparations were in full swing for Junior's homecoming.

"You know how he likes chocolate fudge with black walnuts! And I have saved enough ration coupons to get an extra five pounds of sugar." To be real truthful the sugar coupon came from Junior's personal ration book. Mothers were supposed to turn in all coupon books when a member of the household left home. She really intended to do that, but the extra book came in so handy that she just never got around to doing it. She would relinquish it immediately after his furlough, she promised herself.

"And Alden," she continued with her instructions, "would you drive me into town and to the A & P this afternoon?"

"I will, I will, Mom," one of the twins quickly offered.

"No, Mom, let me," the other chimed in.

"My goodness, you boys don't even have a driver's license!"

"But, we can still drive," they both said in unison, like identical twins do. It was true, like most farm boys, they knew how to drive. But, for the two of them, driving a vehicle was restricted to the farm only. They would be sixteen two days after Christmas when Dad had promised he would take them to the county seat to get their licenses.

It was Saturday and they knew there would be additional chores to do if they were left at home. It seemed as though Dad always found something extra for them to do in the barn. After their chores were done, they would much rather be upstairs in their room building model airplanes and dreaming about the day they could fly away from the farm. Or across the road at the neighbors talking about airplanes, or fixing a flat tire on the family bicycle, or just about anywhere or anyplace other than the barn.

Alden was eager to drive her to town. That meant he was exempt from additional barn work. He backed the well-worn 1934 Chevy sedan close to the 50-gallon gas barrel which, because of war rationing, was to be used for farming only. Farm gas for the truck and tractor was not to be used in the family automobile. This was a rule that often went unheeded on the Bradford farm.

He pulled out a special stick stored near the barrel, wiped it on his shirt sleeve to make sure it was clean and inserted it into the gas tank of the car. The gas gauge, like many other parts of the old car, did not work and this was the only way of knowing if gas was needed. Any automobile repairs would have to wait until after the war. There were simply no parts to buy.

When the stick was pulled out, the height of the wet mark determined if additional gas was needed. Low it was, so Alden withdrew a few gallons in an old kerosene can and carefully poured it into the tank of the car.

Clara had all the ration books in hand, one for each of the children, plus her own, Dad's and Grandma's, ten in all.

The weekly *Eaton Rapids Journal* listed which stamps to use for each individual product. This week's paper listed that stamps G, H, and J for processed food were good through the 20th of the month. Stamps V, W and X were good for the same period for meat, cheese, butter, fats, canned milk and fish. Stamp 30 in book 4 was good for five pounds of sugar. Stamp 18 in book 1 and number 1 airplane stamp in book 3 were good for a pair of shoes. Holders of either an A-10, B, B1, C or a C1 gas sticker were entitled to two gallons of gas.

Not only did Clara have to concern herself with the proper ration stamp from the correct book, but she had to keep in mind that although food prices were frozen, she did not always have enough money to buy the needed food. Ever since they lost their farm during the depression of the early 1930's, it seemed that there was never enough money to cover the essentials for the growing family. After losing the farm, they moved to a rental farm for a few years before putting a small down payment on this farm.

The farm included 80 tillable acres of good soil, but the buildings were in desperate need of repair, renovation or razing. Regardless of its condition, the farm was theirs. It is a man's life-long dream to own a piece of land. The farm provided the basic food needed. Growing a garden, canning fruits and vegetables, raising chickens for eggs and meat, and at least a hog or two for bacon, lard, sausage and chops, provided basic staples. Of course, the cows produced all the milk the family needed. Any extra milk was sold to Miller's Dairy Farms in town to provide a small monthly income. During this difficult time, living on a farm was a lifesaver.

Thanksgiving was next Thursday. That meant the children would be home from school both Thursday and Friday. Thanksgiving dinner would consist of the usual chicken and be observed on Sunday, rather than Thursday, because Winona would be home for the weekend. Her new husband was serving in the army air force, receiving mechanical training in Texas. Three weeks after Thanksgiving, Junior would be home.

On the way to town, Clara counted the money in her purse to make sure there was enough to at least buy 50 pounds of flour and some sugar for baking. It was more common than not to have more ration stamps than money. She felt comfort in knowing the cellar shelves were full of canned fruits and vegetable from last summer's garden.

With a hole in the muffler, the roar of the car engine and the rattle from the loose fitting doors, running boards and fenders, kept them from conversing. The younger children stayed home with Grandma. Alden drove over the bumpy gravel roads with his mother in the seat next to him, both buried in their own thoughts.

Alden's thoughts were focused on his 18th birthday just four days after Christmas. That would mean he would be required to register for the draft. The only way he could avoid being drafted into the army would be to join the navy. He just might do that!

Clara, on the other hand, was deep in thoughts of food preparations, making fudge with walnuts, and Junior's homecoming.

The bleak countryside passed quickly outside the car windows. Clara noticed new stars in the windows of some of the homes they passed. There was a sadness in her heart to see so many of the young men leaving home and going off to war. What an uncertain time. The brush and weeds which had overgrown the roadside were now dry and dead. A withered and twisted reminder that there are seasons in the land as well as seasons of the human spirit. Clara was thinking of the seasons of expectation to come when the winter snow blankets the earth followed by the promise of spring and new hope.

WWII Poster to encourage everyone

to do their best for the War effort.

Chapter 4

Human Guinea Pigs

"Take this to your teacher." Clara handed Jean the paper with her signature, giving approval for her daughter to take part in a government nutritional experiment.

"You're not to have anything to eat this morning. They will give you breakfast after the blood test."

"What is a blood test?" Jean asked.

"The doctor will take a little blood out of your arm and then test it. After a few weeks of eating a special soup they will test it again."

"I don't want my blood tested!" Jean crossed her arms in defiance.

"It's for the war effort. Now hurry, the bus will be here any minute."

The third, fourth and fifth graders were to have a blood test and then eat a nutritious soup, and after an eight-week period the blood would be tested again. This would determine if the "soup" was helpful in improving health. These statistics were then to be used in improving the C-rations given to the soldiers in the battlefields. The goal was to improve the standard field rations and give soldiers more energy and keep them healthy.

The K-rations contained 3000 calories and were designed to be light in weight, small, and easily carried in the soldier's pack. Normally they were to be consumed only under emergency conditions when no other food was available. The decision to send men into battle with the prospect of inadequate daily food was not sanctioned by the doctors. Undernourishment was to play an important part in the poor strength and general health of men in combat. The K- rations lacked bulk and hence left the feeling of being unfed. An improvement to the K-rations had to be found.

Feeding troops in the field has haunted armies over the years. Civil War soldiers carried a biscuit called hardtack, and they constantly suffered scurvy. Fighting men today had to be kept healthy.

The 30 fifth graders lined up in their room on the first floor of the school building. The teacher led them upstairs to the third floor in front of the nurse's room where they fell in line with the third and fourth graders. Under normal circumstances, they were not allowed on the third floor, that's where the big high school kids had their classrooms.

Jean had never been to a doctor before and having a blood test was a completely new experience; nor could she recall any of her family members ever going to a doctor. Clara always tended to the sick and injured children. The well-worn "Doctor Book" on the shelf of the old bookcase held the cures and recommendations for all sorts of illnesses, diseases and injuries. Mother simply flipped through the pages until she found an illness that best fitted the symptoms and applied the recommended cure.

Jean stood in the slow-moving line. Her stomach began to ache. After no breakfast and over an hour ride on the bus, and standing in line for so long, her stomach needed attention. She started to get dizzy and her cheeks were fiery red. The building seemed so warm. Her classmates went in one by one and came out with their left arm folded up at the elbow. A white sterile gauze was clutched in the bend of their arm. Some were crying but they said nothing.

She was next.

She sat on a stool in front of the doctor who wrapped a tight rubber band around her forearm and wiped the bend of her arm with a cold solution.

"Make a fist," he said

She did as she was instructed.

"Now, I'm going to poke this needle in your vein and when I do, you open and close your fist."

She watched every move and was amazed to see the dark maroon blood flow into his tube. She thought blood was red not maroon. Each time her fist was opened and closed, more blood rushed in. It was even warmer in the little nurse's room.

"There." He pulled the needle out and held the vial up to the window light. "No that's not quite enough." The doctor muttered as he reinserted the needle as Jean winced.

When he was finally done he placed a clean white gauze over the punctured vein, and folded her arm up.

"There now, go down to the basement and to the home economics room and have some breakfast."

She started down the four flights of stairs. Her knees seemed so weak. "What a strange feeling," she thought. Everything was going black.

Someone found her passed out on the third flight of stairs. Although she was quickly revived she was helped to the breakfast room.

They were told what a fine contribution they were all making for the war effort and their research to provide better food for the fighting men. Jean thought it was indeed a "sacrifice" rather than a "contribution". But, she was told that it could "save some poor soldier's life"

The daily "soup" they were asked to eat was thin and milky colored. Most youngsters agreed that it was terrible. The few who thought it was good must have come from a family who didn't have much to eat, Jean thought. She gagged it down for the first few days and then had a choice of eating another soup just once a week.

It was a happy time in the cafeteria when the eight-week research period was over. When it came the day for the follow-up blood test, Jean tried to fake an illness in hopes she could stay home from school.

"Oh, Jean, don't be silly!" her mother scolded. "Just turn your head and don't watch."

Jean's "contribution" to the war effort left her traumatized and fearful of needles for the rest of her life. For years she slept with her arms clenched together hiding her veins from any night time invader. She hoped her "sacrifice" saved a life or two.

Later, the government came out with a greatly improved C-ration. It consisted of a variety of canned meats and vegetables, packed in preservatives, along with hard biscuits. C-rations provided 3800 calories a day in battle conditions when it wasn't possible to set up a mess tent. The olive-drab cans were never a hit with the soldiers but a great improvement over the disliked K-rations.

Bill & John wearing their big brother's army hats.

Chapter 5

The Empty Dinner Plate Returns

President Roosevelt's recent "Fireside Chat" warned the nation that the war was going to be a difficult one. "This war" he said "is a new kind of war. It is different from all other wars of the past, not only in its methods and weapons but also in its geography. It is warfare in terms of every continent, every island, every sea, every air-lane in the world." War was everywhere. In February a Japanese submarine shelled the California coast; and in June two German U-boats landed teams of saboteurs on Long Island and near Jacksonville, Florida.

"How far away is Florida?" one of the children asked.

"It's a long way away. Besides they caught them." Clara assured her children that they were safe.

On the first year anniversary of Pearl Harbor, the U.S. Navy launched the battleship New Jersey and eleven other ships. The president urged the people not to listen to rumors but to turn to him to give them the correct facts. "Circulation of such rumors is just another tactic of propaganda intended to drive the American people apart. We will win!" he assured his listeners.

After reading that the United States losses were 44,143 killed, wounded and missing, Clara was saddened as she folded her paper and turned off the radio. As hard as it was, she must put the terrible war news aside and concentrate on Junior's homecoming tomorrow.

Two hours before his expected arrival Dad, Mom and John, who was not yet in school, set out for the train depot to bring their soldier home. Additional time was always allowed when a car trip was scheduled. "Caft" time they called it (case of a flat tire). Alden crafted that saying. Alden the thinker, the mechanical one, could always be counted on for putting an unusual twist to almost any situation. His common sense approach to any problem was valued by the family.

The other children were in school. Alden was left at home to start the evening chores in case the train was delayed and Grandma was at home preparing the homecoming supper.

The ten-mile trip in to Charlotte and the depot was like all other car trips- - without conversation. No one could be heard over the roar of the engine and the racket from the various loose parts of the automobile. The bumpy gravel roads weren't scraped smooth, as they once were before the war, and the car bounced over the rutted washboard road. Even though Alden had patched the hole in the tailpipe, using a tin can he had cut open and wired in place, the rattle of the loose-fitting car parts made any normal conversation inaudible.

When they entered the relatively smooth concrete main street of the city, conversation was resumed. Mostly by Clara. "Slow down, Walter! Don't get so close to that other car! For heavens' sakes look where you are going! The light is red, turn left here!" Clara never held a driver's license and seldom got behind the wheel, but she certainly could direct her husband's driving.

The train was on time and the depot was a center of activity. Young men in their civilian clothes were waiting to board. Standing with them were wives and parents sending their loved ones into military life and an uncertain future. Clara's heart was sad for them.

The passengers started to exit the train. Most were military men. Some were returning home after basic training or boot camp, depending on which branch of the service they were in. Others were on regular furlough before shipping out. With their possessions in a duffel bag slung over their shoulders, the young and robust men were ready to serve their country wherever they would be sent. But more importantly for now, it was home for a short time. Clara recognized a few of them. Howard Umbarger was one of the young men. She had worked years ago with his mother at Horners Woolen Mills. How handsome he looked in his army uniform. But where was Junior?

She stood on her tiptoes to get a better view. She couldn't get closer because of the crowd. Where was he?

Ah, there he was! He stepped into the doorway of the train, pausing to look for his folks. His brown khaki uniform fit like it was tailored and the new stripe on his sleeve indicated he had been promoted to Private first class. With duffel bag slung over his right shoulder, left hand shielding his eyes, he squinted into the late afternoon sun in search of them. And then their eyes connected! He pulled off his hat and waved it high above so they would recognize him. "Silly child," Clara thought. "How could they not recognize him, their own flesh and blood, their firstborn?" He zigzagged through the crowd toward them.

He seemed taller than usual. His smile seemed broader than when he left. His hug seemed tighter than before and his handshake seemed more firm. His beautiful wavy hair was gone, along with his boyish innocence. With his "butch" haircut came somber maturity. He was indeed a seasoned man.

He was home! There would be no talk of the war for fourteen days! He was home, home for Christmas!

Grandma had supper mostly prepared and the children had ten places set at the big oval table when they returned. Grandma tried to hide her special love for her firstborn grandson. Regardless of her feeble attempts, everyone knew he was her favorite. The funny thing is, he was the whole family's favorite.

The children were shy at first, wondering if their big brother was still the same. They wondered if he would take them to town and buy them ice cream like he once did. Alden wondered if the two would go rabbit hunting. They always went pheasant hunting together during the fall season, and often went rabbit hunting when there was a fresh blanket of snow. The twins wanted to surprise him with their driving abilities, even without a license to do so.

"You can't do chores tonight 'cause I'm wearing your boots." Alden interrupted the stillness of the supper table.

Junior pushed back from the table and laughed his old familiar laugh, which was his approval to bring on the conversation and questions. He was the same big brother who had left.

Jean never missed an opportunity to remind him of the time when she was only four. The Bradford children had spent the winter cracking hickory nuts, picking out the meats and placing them in glass quart canning jars.

"Remember, Junior", she began "when Dad took our nutmeats to Millers to sell?"

He smiled his broad grin and knew what was coming next. She had reminded him several times in the past.

The jars of nut meats were sold to Millers Ice Cream plant where they were put in their Hickory Nut Ice Cream. After selling the nuts, Dad returned to the car and handed each waiting hand some coins. Since Jean had filled more jars than the others, she was given a folded up dollar bill.

She had never seen a dollar bill before and couldn't help but show her disappointment. She carefully unfolded the paper dollar hoping to find at least a nickel or even as much as a quarter wrapped inside.

Now eleven years old, she knew the value of a dollar.

"Remember you traded with me for fifty cents?"

Junior rummaged around in his wool khaki paints pocket and handed her another fifty cent piece.

Jean had receiver fifty cents on several other occasions. She knew she had already been well reimbursed, and Junior knew that, too, but never hesitated to dig up another fifty cents whenever the story resurfaced.

Grandma hustled about clearing up the supper table while the others talked and laughed with Junior. He showed them how to salute, how to march and talked about how important it was to keep the camp clean and neat. "One of my buddies was caught throwing a cigarette butt on the ground and was ordered to dig a hole six feet deep to bury it!"

The family was once again back together talking, laughing, enjoying one another. They were all there except Winona, and she would be home on Saturday.

War was put on the back burner at the Bradford farm for fourteen days.

Chapter 6

The Telegram

Clara straightened the flag in the window. The frost on the glass clouded the view of the single blue star. It was bitterly cold. Even though she had stuffed newspaper in the cracks of the loose-fitting window, the draft filtered through and caused the lace curtains to sway with the dance of the wind. For only a moment the morning sun burst through the cloudy sky sending long shadows across the new blanket of snow. It was barely daylight. The wind sent swirls of snow twirling about the yard. The flag shivered from a gust of wind. She put an extra chunk of wood in the living room stove, wanting to send more warmth up its stovepipe to the bedroom above where Junior slept.

Dad, Alden, Kyle and Lyle were in the barn doing the morning milking. They would be in for breakfast soon and then the twins would get ready for school while Dad and Alden completed the chores. Jean and Bill would be getting up soon to get ready for the school bus. Next year John would be among the rest of the children going off to school, but for now he slept peacefully curled up under several quilts.

Dad, as always, built the fire in the living room stove and the kitchen range before leaving the house for the barn. The heat from the range was beginning to warm the kitchen. The floor creaked under each step. Clara removed the black cast iron griddle from its storage behind the kitchen stove and placed it on the top surface to start heating. The coffee pot was filled with cold water, and four tablespoons of ground coffee was added before putting it on to boil. The stove heated evenly. She then got the crockery bowl containing the pancake starter from the shelf in the pantry. This was the same ritual as every other morning.

By the time the chores were done, a stack of pancakes had been piled high on the platter keeping hot in the warming oven above the cooking surface of the stove. A spider of fresh bacon was also fried brown and crisp. The appetizing aroma drifted through the frigid house, waking those who were not already up. Bacon, or meat of any kind, was served only for special occasions. Having Junior home was indeed a special occasion.

He had only been home for a few days. Winona was home on Saturday and Sunday; her presence completed the family circle. Clara laughed and smiled more than she had since the war started. Junior spent most of his days at home but did manage to visit his friends, Horace Whittum, Ivan Dodge and Garfield Dowding, who were still at home and had not been drafted yet. He slept in late and enjoyed his mother's "good home-cooked food," as he called it. "It sure beats the mess hall!" he added. He took all the children to the show in town featuring Fred Astaire and Joan Leslie in *The Sky's the Limit* . The Bradford family took up a whole row of seats in the Capitol theater on Main Street. At twenty-five cents for adults and nine cents for children, Junior paid the cashier one dollar and twenty-seven cents for the seven of them.

The cedar Christmas tree was in place in the corner of the living room. Set in a rusted pail and wired in place, it was decorated with shiny glass ornaments and handmade garlands of colored paper. Jean went with the neighbors when they cut their tree and picked out one for the Bradford family. It was tradition that their Swan neighbor to the north opened his cedar woods for the neighbors to select their Christmas trees.

Before leaving for school Kyle and Lyle pumped a fresh pail of water and split and carried in extra wood for the kitchen range. They put on their identical flannel shirts and clean overalls just in time to catch the bus.

Clara busied herself with the final Christmas baking. Christmas was only three days away and she wanted everything to be just perfect. Eva, Dad's only sister, had invited them to join their family on Christmas day for dinner and a game or two of Pedro before evening chores.

She was humming the newest Christmas song, "I'm Dreaming of a White Christmas." She smiled to herself realizing she was not dreaming of a white Christmas at all. They already had about two feet of snow. Junior was in the living room reading a Zane Grey old west adventure. John sat at the kitchen table pretending to read, too, and Grandma was sorting beans for supper. The creak of the floor as Clara went from oven to table was rhythmic as she placed the big yellow sugar cookies on the baking sheet, positioned it in the oven and removed the baked ones. Back and forth, back and forth.

The impatient honking of the mailman's horn broke the tranquility.

"Whatever does he want?" Clara spoke out loud.

"I'll see what he wants, Mom!" Without a coat, Junior ran to the honking mailman's car.

He returned with a yellow envelope, address to him from the War Department. It was a telegram! The family had never gotten a telegram before. Clara stopped her work and stood close to him while he opened the unfamiliar envelope.

"I gotta go back, Mom- - -as soon as I can. It says to report to camp immediately!"

"Are you sure?" Clara took the telegram from his hand in disbelief.

It was true, he was to report back to camp immediately.

"I don't believe it! It's not true! They can't do this!" She sobbed.

Clara sat at the kitchen table and held her head in utter disappointment. "How could this be?" she muttered over and over. She wondered what war events were taking place to call for his premature return? She hadn't listened to the news since he came home. What was happening? Why must he return two days before Christmas? Would this terrible war ever end?

"The war won't last long, Mom." he consoled her. "I'll be home when it's over."

Chapter 7

The Fireside Chat

Regardless of how devastated Clara felt, she must pull herself together and go on for the other children. After returning from taking Junior to the train depot, she somehow forced herself to continue with plans for Christmas tomorrow. The fudge with walnut meats that she planned to bring out on Christmas morning for the whole family was wrapped in wax paper and placed in the box along with the cookies, and given to Junior as he boarded the train. She roasted the leftover nutmeats and packaged them for his enjoyment as well. A new Zane Grey novel wrapped in bright red tissue-paper and tied with a string was placed in the box, too. It was meant to be under the Christmas tree for him to open on Christmas day.

She hardly had enough sugar left to make more candy or cookies. "Keep the home fires burning" were his last words as he boarded the train. Tall, handsome and smiling his broadest smile, he put on a brave front for his parents. She must find the ingredients to make more for the children. "I wonder if I will ever see him again?" she allowed herself to think. The one-half pound, or one cup of sugar, rationed for each person each week was scarcely enough for any extra cooking like making candy. She must find enough sugar somewhere. Before the war and food rationing she would simply run across the road and borrow a cup or two from the neighbor. But, now, with sugar so scarce, one couldn't borrow from the neighbors who barely had enough for their own family.

She must concentrate on tomorrow. She managed to gather two cups of sugar by dumping the sugar bowl and cleaning out the seams of the sugar bag. That would be enough for one batch of fudge. Dad could go without sugar in his coffee until next week when the succeeding ration stamp would go into effect.

Grandma washed the supper dishes while the children helped with the fudge making as best they could. Lyle and Kyle sat on the kitchen floor near the warmth of the range, with the flat irons turned upside down between their knees, cracking walnuts and removing the stubborn meats. Jean measured the cocoa and milk. Alden cut extra wood for the range, Bill and John were enticed to go to bed early before Santa arrived. Junior had left small packages for the family's Christmas.

The fudge came to a boil and the aroma filled the kitchen. Clara cooked it until a drop of the mixture placed in a cup of cold water formed a soft ball. The black walnut meats were stirred in before pouring it into a greased pan to harden.

Clara dried her hands on the corner of her apron, left the kitchen to sit near the radio in the living room to hear the President's Christmas Eve fireside chat. She never missed his weekly broadcast.

"My Friends: I have recently returned from extensive journeying in the region of the Mediterranean and as far as the borders of Russia. I have conferred with the leaders of Britain and Russia and China on military matters of the present, especially on plans for stepping-up our successful attack on our enemies as quickly as possible and from many different points of the compass.

On this Christmas Eve there are over ten million men in the armed forces of the United States alone. One year ago 1,700,000 were serving overseas. Today, this figure has been more than doubled to 3,800,000 on duty overseas. By next July first that number overseas will rise to over 5,000,0000 men and women."

So, that is why Junior was called back early. They were stepping up the attack.

She turned the radio off and picked up the *Eaton Rapids Journal*, before going to bed. She read where D.G. Miller and E.F. Mix, along with Mr. and Mrs. George Miller, left Eaton

Rapids for a trip down the Mississippi in Mr. Miller's 40-foot luxury Chris Craft Cruiser on a holiday.

Clara folded the paper and looked about her meager surroundings. Bits and pieces of shabby furniture arranged here and there in the chilly living room. She wondered what it would be like to be on a leisurely cruise down the river in a luxury boat instead of worrying about her son soon to be shipped out, and scraping together enough sugar to make candy for Christmas.

Dad banked the fire in the parlor stove while Clara went upstairs to check on her sleeping children. She gently tucked the covers around them while saying a silent prayer to keep them all safe- - each and every one of them, those sleeping here, Winona in Battle Creek and Junior on a troop train somewhere en route to an unknown destination. The children were her luxury cruise, they brought her so much joy. Cruising down the Mississippi could not be more scenic nor pleasurable than watching your children sleep safely and soundly in their warm beds each night.

Tomorrow they would all go to Aunt Eva and Uncle Harry Thuma's for Christmas dinner. They all loved going there. Their house was always warm, and the big dining room table would be stretched to its fullest length and covered with a white table cloth. Aunt Eva always used her best dishes and at each place there would be a little individual glass dish filled with salt where they could dip their celery.

Being with their cousins was a joyous time, too. The Thumas had three children. Two girls, Arlene and Verna were about the same ages as Junior and Winona. Their son, Dean, was near the age of the twins. It was a tradition to alternate holidays with them. If Thanksgiving was spent at the Bradfords, then either Christmas or New Years was spent with the Thuma family.

When the children were younger, it was the custom after dinner for the three cousins, Arlene, Verna and Winona, to get together and practice the latest dance, or sing the most recent songs. There were boys to talk about, with plenty of giggling and other girl talk going on. They were so full of life. The grown-ups played cards, conversed and laughed. The boys would go to the barn and be entertained by Dean, who reenacted the latest Saturday matinee movie. He swung on the hay ropes and fought the enemy with gusto while the Bradford boys sat on a pile of hay watching and applauding.

But this Christmas was different. The girls were all grown up and married. They joined their parents' conversation about the war news and rationed food and not being able to get new tires for the car or replacement parts for farm machinery.

Alden and the twins went to the barn with Dean and helped throw down hay for the cows. Jean and the two younger boys played Old Maid with a new deck of cards Junior had bought for them.

The day ended in time to get at the evening chores. Both families had chores and milking to do.

They parted with the usual hugs and the promise to "See you New Years day!"

Two days after Christmas the twins would turn 16 years old and two days after that Alden would be 18, and then a whole new year would begin. With a heavy heart Clara realized that Alden would be required to register for the draft, and the war news was so grave. As solemn as the outlook seemed, Clara believed that somehow, someway, 1944 would be a better year.

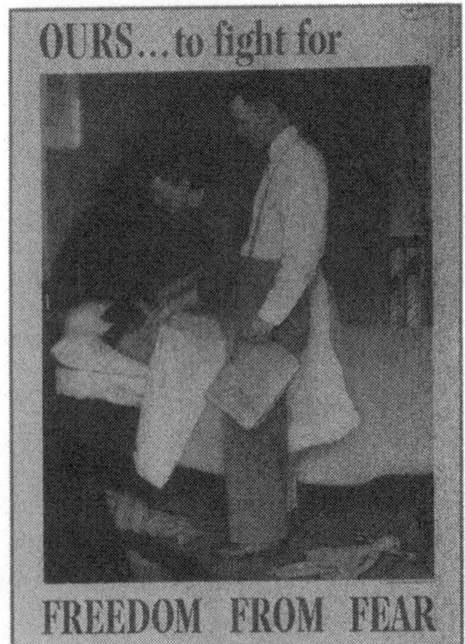

WWII posters to encourage the folks at home

to buy War Bonds for freedom

Chapter 8

Supporting the War Effort

The first *Eaton Rapids Journal* of the new year did not share Clara's optimism. On the front page an article written by the Honorable Robert P. Patterson, Under Secretary of War, titled, "1944 to Decide Future of World," said:

"The greatest strain in history is about to be put upon this country...on labor, on industry, on the entire population. There have been troubles and difficulties in the past and we have, in the main, overcome them. But the most difficult job of all lies ahead. That is the drive to Victory!

"War in a democracy is, and must be, a partnership. It has been repeatedly proved in combat that the soldier who knows not only what he has to do but why he has to do it is the best soldier and the most dogged and determined fighter. He is a partner in the battle strategy.

"Civilians, too, are partners in the war, and none more so then our men and women who make the weapons with which our soldiers fight. Victory is ahead but it is the considered judgment of our military leaders that we still have a long, hard fight.

"The war has taken a turn in our favor. Recent campaigns have been successful. It would be impossible to overestimate the part that American-made equipment has played in these victories.

"Industry and labor have done a magnificent production job in this war. I know of no parallel to it. But we must do better and better. The big operations, the decisive operations, lie ahead. This is no time for patting ourselves on the back. The job ahead is too hard for that.

"We shall all carry a heavy burden during the coming twelve months. It will be a costly year, costly in blood and men, but it is a year that will determine the future of the world. The stakes are worth fighting for. On my trip to the Pacific I saw many things. I saw the lonely graves in the jungle. I saw the wounded and sick in the hospitals. I saw thousands of brave American and Australian soldiers winning under the hardest conditions. We have pledged those men and the men fighting on other fronts the full resources of the nation to support them. We must not fail."

Every patriotic person agreed. We all must do our part to bring this terrible war to victory. What more could Clara do? She had sent one son and soon another would go. Three of her brothers were already serving in the army. She wept with her daughter as her husband left his bride to serve in the army airforce. She bought less than the quantity of food designated by the ration stamps; she raised a garden, canned all sorts of fruits and vegetables to feed her family and not buy food, so the service men would have enough to eat, just like the paper asked. She saved any leftover grease in a can on the back of the kitchen range and turned it in at the meat market to make ammunition for the Yanks. She lowered the windows shades during every air-raid drill. The family never took a Sunday ride in order to save gas. She saved string, paper and any little piece of metal, and the children scoured the fields and roadways picking milkweed pods to be used for life jackets. She was never enticed by black-market items; if she wasn't entitled to it she didn't consider buying it. What more could she do? Remorsefully, she never bought a war bond. However, an extra dime would be found from time to time for the children to buy a savings stamp at school and stick it in a special book. When the book was filled it could be turned in for a $25.00 war bond. During the entire war years the children never had enough money to purchase sufficient stamps to buy a single bond. Even when their stamps were combined, there was not enough.

She wished she could buy bonds. Everywhere one looked there was a plea to buy a bond. At school, posters in the store windows and ad after ad in the paper urged everyone to buy stamps and bonds. On the front page of the Journal a war poster urged “Bring Your Boy Home! Back the Attack with Bonds.” “Eaton Rapids School Children Buy Two Jeeps,” was another article. “$2,297 in stamps and bonds were purchased, which is enough to buy two jeeps.” it said.

“How can I do more?” she asked herself. Perhaps she could find enough time to do some knitting for the Red Cross. The paper urged knitters to volunteer for the war program and knit sweaters. Or, perhaps she could help roll bandages. She could go to church, like Mayor Hiram Webster proclaimed, and pray for our Yanks. Even as busy as she was she could find a way to do more. She would do her best, just like everyone else, to move the U.S. closer to victory and bring the Yanks back home.

Chapter 9

Winter Pleasure - - Ice Skating on the Pond

The winter of 1944 was extremely cold. The snow came early and the wind seemed to never rest. One good thing about the wind, it kept the pond swept clean of snow exposing the clear blue ice and freezing it deeply. The alluring ice beckoned ice skaters to put on their skates and be the first to make marks on its clear, smooth surface.

The Bradford kids clamored to the cellarway for the ice skates. They had been hanging there on nails since the ice melted last spring. It was always a jumble to find a matching set with straps that were whole and did not need to be repaired. The skates were adjustable to fit growing shoe sizes, and those who were not lucky enough to have a pair simply took turns with the others. The younger ones usually did not have skates, so they were pulled around and around the pond on the family's only sled by those who did.

Alden carried the only skate key on a string around his neck, and it was his responsibility to tighten the clamps on the skates to the shoe soles of the others. Often a skate would come unclasped and the skater would take a hard fall on the ice. They dreamed of the day they could have shoe skates with high tops and laces like some of the other richer kids had.

"I'll race ya to the other side!" one of the twins challenged the other. And they were off in a hail of chipped ice and hearty yells. "Come on, slow poke, what ya waiting for?"

Often on a sunny Saturday afternoon all the neighborhood kids joined the Bradfords at the pond. They played crack-the-whip, tag, held races, jumped the sled and other objects, hit a tin can across the ice with a small limb from a nearby tree, laughed, shouted and played until the sun went down.

As darkness gathered it was a reminder that the boys had chores to do. They unclasped their skates and headed for the house with a promise they would return after supper when the milking was done, if the moon was bright. The other children unclasped their skates, too, and headed for home. It wasn't near as much fun without the older boys to play with.

The full moon reflected on the white snow making the night almost as bright as day. The boys quickly finished the milking and rushed out to the pond. They gathered up small sticks and wood from Clara's kindling box and took a few matches and some paper to start a fire on the edge of the pond. A large log was dragged from the other side of the pond and soon a roaring fire was underway. The wind was still. The smoke from the fire spiraled straight up. The night was so very still and the sounds magnified through the night air. In the distance they heard the whistle of the Lansing-to-Jackson freight on its night run.

One by one the children came back for more fun on the ice. Without arguing too much, the Bradford kids took turns with their skates. The frolicking continued until Clara called from the kitchen door. “Come on in kids, it’s bed time.”

When they stomped the snow off their feet and came through the kitchen door, hot cocoa was waiting on the big black cast-iron cookstove .

She enjoyed seeing her children happy and healthy with red cheeks and red runny noses. “Do you have a hankie?” was her question. Which really meant, “stop your snuffing and blow your nose!”

“Put your wet mittens on the oven door to dry,” she instructed as she helped hang up coats, hats and scarfs over nails on the wall in back of the big kitchen range. “Here, take this and help the young ones dry their noses.”

The laughter and clamor continued. Sitting around the big kitchen table with the oilcloth cover, they sipped hot cocoa and warmed themselves, both inside and out. They warmed their flannel pajamas near the stove before scampering off to bed. It was too late for the usual children's story read by Grandma.

The house was so still after the children went to bed. This was the only time of day one could hear the ticking of the clock.

Dad came in from the barn after bedding down the cattle and checking the horses. "Here, Dad, take off your boots and put your feet here on the oven door." Clara moved the wet mittens aside and arranged a kitchen chair for him to sit on. His feet seemed to suffer most during the cold winter months. He slipped off his rubber boots, removed his gray wool socks with red bands around the top, and placed his feet on a towel spread on the open oven door.

"Oh, Buster, that feels so good." He relaxed in the chair.

He had spent the day in the woods cutting down trees, cross sawing the bigger logs and cutting limbs and smaller branches with the double-bladed ax. He and the older boys then loaded the wood onto the bobsled for the trip back to the house. Once there it would be split in proper lengths and piled in two piles. One for the kitchen range which contained the smaller wood, and the other of larger pieces that would fit in the pot-bellied living room stove.

Clara picked up the *Eaton Rapids Journal* . The front page announced that Eaton Rapids would never surrender! "We will do what it takes to win this war." Turning the page she read where Dennis Miller scraped the snow off the ice near the dam and strung up electric lights for the children in town to ice skate on the Grand River.

Chapter 10

The Sugar Bush

When the roads became too muddy for the school bus to get through, it also meant maple syrup time. As the days started getting warmer and snow began to melt, the roads became a river of mud, making them impassable for automobiles. But the best part of the early spring season is when the sap moves up from the roots to the branches of the maple trees. It's sugarin' time!

Only horses and wagon could get back to the sugar bush through the long muddy lane. First the twins and Alden went with Dad to the "bush" to tap the trees. They drilled small holes in the trees, inserted a spile and hung a shiny two-gallon pail beneath. As soon as the holes were drilled and metal tubes inserted, the sap began to flow.

"Split, splat,split splat," the sweet sap dropped into the empty pails.

That was the loudest sound heard in the stillness of the woods. Occasionally a squirrel scolded from a limb above, while the sound of the dripping sap echoed throughout the dormant woods.

The floor of the woods was covered with last fall's leaves, forming a cushion to walk from tree to tree. The boys ran through the woods like spring colts, inhaling the fresh cool air, enjoying the warm sun and racing from tree to tree. One drilled, using a brace-'n-bit, the other inserted the hollow metal spile and hung the pail.

"Hey Kyle, how can you tell a maple from an oak tree?'

"Don't know for sure, Lyle!"

"Well then, what would you get if you tapped an oak tree?" Lyle asked his twin.

"I guess you would get a-corn!" Kyle responded with a chuckle.

"Put a hole on each side of that one.- - she's a big one." Dad instructed.

Any tree eight to ten inches in diameter was large enough to tap, but the large older trees were tapped twice and sometimes three times.

Clara packed a lunch of fried-egg sandwiches so they could get the job done before returning to the house for evening chores. The sun filtered through the branches of the leafless trees and warmed their backs as they sat on the trunk of a fallen tree to eat. She had baked bread yesterday and this morning sliced it about an inch thick and spread each slice with yellow butter and golden mustard before positioning a fried egg.

"I've decided to join the navy, Dad." Alden broke the silence.

"I figured you would." Dad responded. Dad never had many words to say. He did a lot more thinking than he did talking. But, he knew Alden would be drafted into the army if he did not join the navy. Each evening he read the papers and listened to the news and believed Alden would stand a better chance of surviving in the navy.

"When will ya leave?" Dad asked

"Probably by fall," Alden responded.

After the trees were all tapped they gathered up wood for the fire in the morning under the big open-top metal tank to begin the process of boiling down the sap. It takes 40 to 50 gallons to make a gallon of maple syrup, so that takes lots of wood and a lot of boiling.

The next morning Alden stayed back to do the chores, while the twins and Jean boarded the wagon with Dad and headed for the sugar bush. Jean's job was to stir the boiling sap and keep the fire going.

It was barely daylight. The dirt lane was bumpy from the now frozen ruts, made the evening before. Each breath formed a white puffy cloud. Dad stood at the front of the wagon steadying himself against the front rack of the wagon. With the reins in his hands, he spoke to the horses to gee and haw in an attempt to maneuver the wagon over the smoothest part of the lane. He had a special way with horses. The three children bounced and jolted about as they sat on the bed of the wagon.

The sugar bush was at the end of the fenced-in lane. Along either side lay the fields waiting for the ground to warm and spring tilling to begin. Here and there portions of green wheat were revealed where the snow had melted. Row after row of brown stubble from last fall's corn crop lined the next field. That field would be turned under and oats planted this spring. Spring lay in wait. Last year's oat field was broadcast with timothy seed in the fall, and a good cover of insulating snow would give it a head start for an early summer cutting. It would then grow back for another cutting late in the summer or early fall. If the weather was just right, maybe even three cuttings could be harvested from the same field.

Dad was eager to get onto the land and mold it with his plow and drag, to conform it to his desires before feeding it fertile seeds. A farmer is a special kind of person. One who finds enjoyment working from sunup to sundown tilling the soil, sweating in the hot summer sun and being chilled by the frozen earth in winter. His reward is the joy to see what the ground will bring forth under his and the Almighty's hands. Dad was that kind of a man. None of his children were.

Upon arrival, the twins unhitched the wagon and hitched the team to the stone boat that held the big oblong stock tank. Dad and Jean gathered more wood and stacked it nearby for use when the fire burned down.

Boiling down was the best part. The horses wound their way throughout the sugar bush while Dad and the boys dumped the full pails of sweet watery sap into the tank. The pail was replaced to be filled again and gathered the following morning.

Years before, a fireplace was built using stones to contain the fire and support a long metal pan on top. The pan was about two feet wide, ten feet long and eight inches deep. After Dad built the fire the boys dumped the sap into the long pan.

The stir stick was long with a wooden blade on the end. The blade was much like the one on the road grader, only a lot smaller. Jean gently swished the sap back and forth, scraping the bottom of the pan and being very careful not to spill a drop over the sides.

"Don't let it burn! Scorched maple syrup tastes bad!" Dad warned.

It seemed to take forever to come to a boil and when it started to boil there was also skimming to do. The brown colored foam formed on the top had to be skimmed off. The thick, white steam from the evaporating sap wafted through the tranquil woods, spreading its sweet aroma. The boiling continued all day and wood had to be constantly added to keep the fire hot.

Lunch today was eaten while sitting on stones near the fire. Along with fried egg sandwiches, a green-glass canning jar filled with coffee, with sugar and cream already added, was their beverage. It was wrapped in last week's *Eaton Rapids Journal* to keep it as warm as possible. Clara also sent along a whole cherry pie. The cherries had been picked last summer, canned and placed in the basement for a purpose like today.

After lunch more wood was gathered and cut or sawed to the correct size. The pails of sap had all been dumped and while Dad searched for more fallen trees, the twins took the opportunity to climb high into a huge oak tree. They dared one another to climb just a little higher. It was the tallest tree in the woods, with limbs spaced just so to make climbing inviting. There was freedom up there. The view was spectacular looking over the tops of the other trees and seeing their house in the distance. The tree swayed in the wind. The wonder of the endless blue sky stretched before them, magnifying their imagination and beckoning them to explore the vast unknown. The immense height, the sun on their faces and the gentle sway to the beat of the wind, temporarily fulfilled some kind of a longing they could not understand nor could they explain.

It was getting late. The sun was sinking in the west and it was getting colder, when Dad declared the syrup was thick enough and ready to dip into a clean ten-gallon milk can.

"If Buster thinks it needs more evaporating, she can do it on the kitchen range before she cans it. "

The children never knew why he called their mother, his wife, "Buster." She always called him "Dad."

Dad whittled a small paddle from a tree limb for each of the children. This was to be used to "lick the pan" for every speck of sweet, sticky, golden syrup that might be left. Sort of like scraping the bowl after the cake mixture had been placed in the baking pans- - only this was a ten foot pan!

Once home, Clara boiled the syrup down more and sealed it in quart jars for later use. It would be used for syrup on their morning pancakes and some would be boiled down even more for maple sugar candy. It would save a great deal on their precious ration of sugar. Dad often placed a chunk of the candy in his coffee when the ration of sugar was all used up.

Maple syrup season only lasted for a week the spring of 1944. The sun came out and the trees budded much earlier than usual. When that happens the sap must go to nourish the leaves and keep the tree healthy for another sappin' season. Dad got out onto the land he loved early. Clara said an early spring was a good sign. A sign the future would be better. Perhaps it meant the war would end.

WWII Lights Out poster to encourage everyone to turn their lights out especially during "blackouts."

Chapter 11

May Day - Black Out

May first, or May Day as most folks called it, was a time to gather flowers, make baskets and secretly set them on the neighbors' doorstep. Or, better still, if the handle of the basket was strong enough, hang it on the front door knob. Then knock on the door and run and hide behind a tree or shrub. From their hidden vantage point, the children could watch with delight as their gift was received.

It was also the day that signaled kicking off shoes and digging bare toes in the cool earth. A day to celebrate the fertility of the land and all living things. It was a bit colder this May first, but spring was not far behind. Maple syrup season was over and the pink mayflowers carpeted the floor of the woods. It was too early for the white lilies, the yellow adderstongues, and the pink honeysuckles that would spring up among the may flowers. The golden cowslips and deep blue flags, grew in the bogs east of the house, were awaiting more sunshine before they celebrated the season by poking their colorful heads from their winter slumber.

Even if there was a war going on and a blackout scheduled for this evening, the Bradford children would not let that dampen their spirits.

"Jean, you mix up some paste." "Ya, Jean, make some paste. "The twins ordered their sister in identical twin fashion.

"Lyle, get the wallpaper book!" Kyle was giving directions now.

"You either have to add more flour or dump some of the liquid out," Mom cautioned Jean with special emphasis on "not to waste a drop."

One would think as many times as she had mixed flour and water together to make a paste that she could do it without any instructions. After several attempts of adding more flour she got the right consistency.

Selecting the most beautiful wallpaper sample from the book was not an easy task. Since there would be only three baskets made for the Swan neighbors, it was difficult to agree on only three patterns. The flowers and designs were each as lovely as the other.

After much wrangling the three were chosen and gently ripped from their binding. Each was rolled into a pointed cone and pasted along one side. A strip of paper was pasted across the open top to serve as a handle.

While the baskets dried, the children went to the woods to gather mayflowers from the abundant number found there. When they returned, they also brought the cows home for the evening milking. Sometimes they would come to the barn on their own, but most of the time they had to be fetched.

Since the twins had chores to do, the three younger children delivered the May baskets.

"Now you get home before dark," Clara warned "because tonight is another blackout drill."

The children placed the baskets over the doorknobs, knocked and hid behind the nearest tree. The neighbors came to the door and pretended not to see the children who were giggling behind the tree. "Oh, thank you!" they shouted to the "empty" yard. The children learned the joy of giving to others and in making people smile. They also learned that it isn't necessary to take credit for a good deed to be warmed by it.

They bounded home just as darkness was gathering. They were full of laughter and good-hearted bantering. "They never saw us, Mom!" John happily reported.

She tussled his heavy head of hair.

"Can you help me pull the shades down?" Clara asked her children.

"Why do we have to have a blackout?" John asked.

"We have to practice in case we are bombed like the Germans are doing in England."

"Will we get bombed?" Bill asked.

"No, we won't be bombed," she assured her children. "We just need to turn off our lights as much as we can and make sure the shades are down so not a bit of light gets out." Even the tiniest bit of light could be spotted from an airplane at nighttime in total darkness.

Dad commented that if the United States were to be bombed, they would hardly pick the countryside even if they did get through our protected borders. Detroit, the arsenal of democracy, would be a likely spot to be attacked.

The air raid warden, Cecil Swan, the neighbor to the north, drove his car around the countryside to make sure everyone was conforming to the war rules. Not only were all the lights to be off or concealed with black shades, no automobiles were to be on the road for the period of the drill. The goal was to create total darkness so the enemy could not locate a target to attack.

May Day and a blackout drill all in the same day. One to celebrate new life and the other to preserve life.

Chapter 12

Dandelions Harbor Springtime on the Farm

Nothing compares to springtime on the farm. Magic happens. It is the time when the bare dormant trees burst forth with a palette of pastel colors. Shades of pink, green and blue cover the drab and dead-looking branches of winter. The roadside sings with a chorus of color embellished by the sun. Every shrub, bush, weed and blade of grass has taken on a new rainbow of life. The water from the early morning rain runs freely through the ditches, eager to be on its way. It is enchanting! The air seems lighter, too, like it had just been scrubbed clean.

Clara stepped onto the weathered and rickety porch. She closed her eyes and took in a deep breath, exhaled slowly and then took in another and another. Welcome spring, exhale winter, welcome spring, exhale winter.

While nature burst in its glorious renewal, the farm animals felt the new surge of life, too. The horses moved faster with renewed spirit, the milk cows fairly ran to the pasture to feast upon the new green grass they instinctively knew awaited them.

The pigs oinked and rooted about looking for a patch of dry soil to rest upon in the sun, and the chickens scratched about in the loosened dirt looking for spring insects.

Spring is the time for farm animals to reproduce themselves. There are baby calves being born, a litter of pigs taking their first breath, and new born kittens with eyes sealed shut -- it all happens in the barn. The setting hens refuse to leave their nests hidden in the haymow, under the corn crib or in the granary. Their instinct is to set on the collection of eggs they have laid until they are hatched. It happens every spring.

The gentle breeze tugged at Clara's hair, neatly pinned to the back in a bun, and teased at the hem of her freshly ironed apron. Her face was turned directly into the healing rays of the sun. It felt so good. It washed away the stresses in her life for a therapeutic minute or two. She would like to fling off her shoes and wiggle her toes in the warmth of the good earth.

The sharp chirping of a robin caused her to open her eyes. He was calling his mate to a place where angleworms were sure to be close to the surface.

Clara smoothed her apron and returned to the house to begin her work. The concern for the safety of her oldest son, somewhere in England, and worry for her second son who would soon be leaving, were always in her thoughts.

"There is work to be done, to be done,

There's a war to be won, to be won"

She sang the old WWI song as she proceeded to tend to the injured piglet in the box beneath the kitchen range. It wasn't uncommon to find an injured or weaker newborn animal under the warmth of the stove receiving Clara's healing care. When the animal was well enough to get out of the box, it was strong enough to go back to the barn and its mother.

"Shall I gather some dandelions for supper?" Grandma asked.

"They should be about the right size. Look along the fence row," Clara suggested.

Dandelions are best before their brilliant yellow flowers bloom. Grandma would take a pail and knife and dig out the delicious tender wild greens by the roots, wash them in the tin wash tub that hangs on the porch, and then they would be ready to boil for supper. Sprinkled with vinegar was how the family liked them best.

The children would be home an hour earlier from school today. The nation's time had been changed to "war time" or "fast time" as some called it, which meant everyone set their clocks an hour ahead. Everyone, except the Bradfords. They got up before sunup and went to bed after sundown. It didn't much matter what the clock said. War time meant to them that the school bus came earlier than usual. The time would go back to "standard war time" or "slow time" on September 30th. The purpose was to save electricity for the war effort and to allow people to get home from work early enough to plant and tend to a victory garden. Everyone was urged to grow enough food to feed themselves and their family in order to save food for the Yanks.

You could set your clock by Dad's appearance at the dinner table- - twelve noon. He didn't need a watch. When the sun was directly overhead and there were no shadows, Dad knew it was time to eat. The horses did too. They fairly ran back to the barn after being unhitched from the heavy farm machinery.

"Dinner ready, Buster?"

Dinner was always ready at noon, slow time.

Because of "fast time" the farm news was broadcast at eleven o'clock now instead of twelve. The prices of livestock and grain were heard by Clara and Grandma. Anything important enough they would pass along to Walter. Dinner was eaten during *Kate Smith Speaks* news and commentary program. She began each broadcast belting out her theme song *When the Moon Comes Over the Mountain* and ended each program with a rousing *God Bless America!*

After dinner Dad went back to the field, leaving Clara to listen to her favorite afternoon programs. *Our Gal Sunday* -- where a girl from a little mining town in the west searches for happiness. Followed by *Helen Trent* who answers the question; can a woman find happiness at 35 and even beyond? And then *Ma Perkins*, brought to you by Oxydol, the announcer boomed. They provided a diversion for housewives and allowed them to dream and think of other things for fifteen minutes at a time. It was a popular escape from the war, rationing and hard work.

It would be a busy spring, just like every spring on the farm. In addition to the usual planting, cultivating, gardening and spring house cleaning, Lyle and Kyle joined the 4-H calf club. This meant they each must pick out a young heifer from the herd, train and get it ready for the county fair in the fall. The neighbors gave Bill and John each a baby lamb, which had lost its mother and needed to be bottle fed. The brooder coop needed to be made ready before a shipment of baby chicks arrived through the mail next week. It was, indeed, a busy spring.

Just before bedtime, Clara and Walter sat down to read for awhile before going to bed. Walter usually read the latest copy of the *Michigan Farmer* magazine while Clara read either the *Eaton Rapids Journal* or the *State Journal.*

Prolonging bedtime, six-year-old Bill asked a final question. "Dad, what did you do today?"

"Oh, nothing," Dad replied without looking up from his reading.

"Well then, how do you know when you're done?"

Dad lowered the magazine and laughed out loud. Bill was puzzled. He went to bed unaware he had said anything funny.

"Dad, look at this!" Clara often read the most important portions of the paper out loud. "It says, Sgt. Keith Stimer has been injured in action in the Pacific. That's Glen and Gladys's son."

"That's a shame."

"And look here. 'A breakfast was given in honor of Stanley Phinney, who will be leaving for Fort Sheridan in Illinois.' That's the Phinney boy from the Fox district," Clara added.

"Oh, my!" she continued, "Tom True passed away. It says he was the Mayor back in 1912."

"Well, that old geezer invented the wagon racks on our wagon. He had a factory where 'The Best Gas Station by a Dam Site' sits today. Too bad, too bad." Dad added

Clara rubbed her tired eyes and Dad yawned. It was 11 o'clock war time, or 10 o'clock slow time. Regardless what time the nation said it was, it was bedtime at the Bradford house.

GAR Island Park during Decoration Day tribute

Chapter 13

Decoration Day on the Island

"Oh, my. It looks like the spirea will bloom in time for Decoration Day. And the lilacs too." Clara was talking to Jean. "Look near the pond for flags." The wild iris grew near swamps, ponds and wet areas.

Gathering flowers and taking them to the cemetery was a family tradition. The white spirea with its long slender limbs, among purple lilacs and bright blue flags with yellow centers, made a beautiful bouquet. The fragrance of the lilacs overpowered the rest.

Placing flowers on baby Geneva's grave was a solemn time. Most of the children never knew her. She died when she was only six-months old. Winona was four and Junior was five when it happened. The other children knew little about their sister, only that she was taken to Ann Arbor for treatment and there was something wrong with her spine and it could not be fixed.

They did know, however, that on each May 30th, Decoration Day, a bouquet of flowers was taken to the Hamlin Township

Cemetery and placed in front of the simple tombstone that read "Geneva Bradford born 1926 - died 1927 at age 6 months."

The first official proclamation of Memorial Day, or Decoration Day as most called it, was issued in 1868 by General John A. Logan, first commander of the Grand Army of the Republic. This order established Decoration Day on the 30th of May and was set aside to show honor to the patriotic dead of the Civil War by decorating their graves and holding solemn ceremonies. Over the years the custom included decorating veterans' graves of all wars, and then spread to decorating the graves of others, not just those of service men.

The schedule of the day's events was found on the front page of the Eaton Rapids Journal. Even though the corn was not completely planted, Clara asked Dad to take her to the cemetery and to the Memorial Day program.

"Judas Priest, Buster, don't ya know there's a war going on?" That was the standard answer for most requests of any kind during the war years.

After a little thought, he smiled and said. "One of the boys will take ya. I can't go this time, I gotta get the rest of the corn planted."

"The parade starts at 1:30. Ray Gulliver is Marshall of the Day. He was Junior's FFA teacher." Clara offered.

She read from the paper. "The lineup will be the Colors and Guard, Veterans of Foreign Wars, American Legion, VFW Auxiliary, American Legion Auxiliary, Service Men, Red Cross, High School Band, City Firemen and School Board members. The events today resembled those of the very first Memorial Day commemorated in Waterloo, New York in 1866. The moving and lengthy services included speeches by General Murray and a local clergyman".

Clara continued to read. "After the parade the program will continue at the G.A.R park where "America" will be sung by those assembled there. An Invocation by Rev. Richard Miles will follow and then a selection sung by the High School Girls Chorus. Lincoln's Gettysburg Address will be recited by honor-student Melvin Montie. The High School Band will follow up with Sousa's "Stars and Stripes Forever." After an address by Rev. Matthew A. Vance, flowers will be strewn on the water in honor of the service men and women who gave their lives. A twenty-one gun salute, the taps and then the band playing "The Star Spangled Banner" will close the ceremonies." "Doesn't that sound interesting, Walter?"

It was much the same routine each year. Clara enjoyed the solemn program, especially strewing the flowers on the river and watching them catch the current and flow downstream and out of sight.

Alden drove his mother and the three younger children to the cemetery and to the Decoration Day observance in town. The twins now had their driver's licenses but their help was needed in the field. The corn must be planted. Dad must wean himself from Alden's dependable help, so he was the one given the task to drive the rest of the family to town.

At the Cemetery, Clara stooped near the little headstone and pulled the weeds and tall grass to clearly expose Geneva's name. Alden dug a hole in the sod large enough to accept the glass canning jar. The other children watched in silence.

"Don't walk on the graves," Clara warned in almost a whisper.

The children wondered why she whispered, but didn't ask. They just knew this was a solemn time and a sad time for their mother who lost her child. She never talked about it, nor did the children ever ask.

She lingered at the little grave after the others had gone back to the car. She fussed with the flowers and added more water from a pump near by. Her feelings were mixed. She mourned for her sweet daughter who would be almost 19 had she lived. And for her firstborn who was over there in harm's way and for Alden who would soon be leaving for the navy and an uncertain future.

She dabbed her eyes with her hankie and returned to the car.

The roar of the engine broke the silence as they drove on into town and to the Decoration Day ceremonies.

It was a very solemn and inspiring program, just as Clara expected. The school band playing The "Star Spangled Banner" sent shivers up her spine. There was not much talking as they departed from the island park. The impressive tribute to the fallen dead could not be overshadowed by trivial conversation, but must be allowed "silent time" to sink deep into one's soul.

Once at home, and the evening chores done, Clara picked up the Journal to finish reading. She noted that graduation would be held on the first day of June in the high school gymnasium. The class of 1944 would receive their diplomas. It would be a joyous but sad time for the young people. A launching time, a beginning of a whole new life. The sad part was that many would be heading for a branch of the armed forces and their future would be put on hold for a while, or perhaps lost in some faraway place.

Chapter 14

Bea and the Cattle Truck

"Buster!" Walter called from the doorway of the barn. "Buster, I'll be out in the barn when Tom comes."

Tom McClure hauled the neighborhood cattle to the Charlotte stockyard in his big stake truck. He would be taking one of the Bradford's cows to market today. That's what happens when a cow stops giving enough milk. There would be a little extra money for a time. Of course, there were always more places for the money to go than there was money. Like the monthly milk check, there was always more month left after the money was gone.

Each time the big truck rattled into the yard Jean met it in the drive hoping Tom's daughter Bea would be with him. She usually was.

The two girls met years before when the Bradfords were new to the neighborhood. Tom drove into the yard to let them know that he did trucking of almost any kind, should they need his services. As the two men talked near the back porch,

Bea clung to her Dad's leg and smiled at Jean, who was also clinging to the security of her father's leg.

The two seemed to have an immediate liking for each other. Bea was a year younger with black hair and green eyes and a continuous smile that beamed a friendly invitation to those she met. They became instant friends.

As Jean had hoped, Bea was with her Dad. She bounded from the passenger seat and the two girls were off to anyplace they could find where they could laugh, talk, and giggle over almost any silly thing.

Over the years they shared their most secret feelings and desires. When they were children they talked about dolls, and riding horses, and swung on the hay rope in the barn. Later, as they grew into adolescents they noticed boys and agreed they were disgusting. They discussed the wearing of their first brassieres, wore lipstick when their mothers did not know, and took a renewed interest in their clothes. As time went on they decided boys were not so disgusting after all and even shared their dreams of who they would someday marry. Early on they vowed to be best friends forever. Bea shared her first bottle of "Evening in Paris" perfume with her best friend. From the cobalt blue bottle with the gold tassel, they put some on their finger tips and dabbed it behind their ears. The glorious fragrance transported them from the bleak farm to the gaily lit streets of Paris.

"Come on, Bea!" called her Dad. The cow was loaded and tied down in the back of the truck. He had several other stops to make before taking his load to Charlotte.

Her visits were never long enough. And when her impatient Dad said "Come on" he meant NOW! Not in five minutes, but right now. It seemed he was always in a hurry.

Leaning out the passenger window Bea called from the moving vehicle, "I'll ride my horse over on Thursday."

It seemed forever before that day came. Jean waited in the front yard and looked from time to time up the road for a horse and rider. As soon as they were spotted, she was off on a run to meet them. "Bea's coming," she called over her shoulder in the direction of the house.

Bea immediately slid from the back of her big brown riding horse, which she rode bareback, and the two of them walked the short distance to the house together.

"I thought you would never get here!" Jean said

"Mom made me do the dishes before I came," Bea answered in disgust.

Bill bounded from the house "Can I ride? Can I ride?" He was fascinated with a spirited, slim-legged riding horse. On the Bradford farm there were only large, stocky work horses who plodded along as if they were pulling a plow when you only wanted to ride them.

The girls helped him up on Trigger's narrow back. While Bea led the horse around and around the yard, Bill imagined he was on the back of a speeding steed, riding alongside of Gene Autry or Roy Rogers, in hot pursuit of the bad guys in the black hats.

The twins and Alden teased Bea about her horse, calling it "a nag." "How many miles do you get per gallon on that ole nag?" they would scoff. She enjoyed their bantering and savored their attention. She, like so many other young girls, was beginning to realize how handsome they were becoming. Jean, on the other hand, hadn't noticed, but guessed her brothers would pass as mediocre.

The girls walked back into the woods and gathered wildflowers and inhaled the perfume from the crabapple tree in the lane. Even the choke cherry tree had a sweet fragrance although its fruit was bitter and not edible. They walked barefoot in the cow paths that had been worn down to sand. Puffs of dust mushroomed around each step. Their conversation centered around the latest songs, a book Bea had read, or a challenge to climb a nearby tree. They were adults one minute and children the next. Their concerns were not of war with its rationing and blackouts and going without, but of being young and full of life.

Bea's stays were never long enough. It seemed the afternoon fairly vanished and it was time for her to get on her horse and head back down the road. The two-mile ride home seemed to take longer than the same distance did coming. But she left with a promise that Jean would walk the distance to her house next week. This tradition of getting together, in one way or another, kept up their entire lifetime.

Guy Kellogg, Clara Bradford's brother, holding the "E" after their plan flew 10,000 sorties (missions) in Itally during WWII.

Chapter 15

The Terrible War

Clara pulled her chair near to the radio with her ear close to the speaker. Reception was not very good tonight because of a storm brewing in the west. It was the President's weekly Fire Side Chat, and even though it was difficult to hear through the crackling static, she strained to listen to the latest war events.

The war news was more hopeful tonight. President Roosevelt announced that Rome had fallen to the American and Allied troops. "The first of the Axis capitals is now in our hands. One up and two to go!" he said.

Clara was relieved to hear the war news was turning in our favor after such a long time. Her brother, Guy, was stationed in Italy. He was the chief of the maintenance crew for a B-17 that had successfully completed 10,000 missions. What a record that must be!

The president seemed to be speaking of an even greater "push" on Germany. "It would be unwise to inflate in our own minds the military importance of the capture of Rome. We shall have to push through a long period of greater effort and fiercer fighting before we get into Germany itself."

The evening news the very next day answered Clara's questions about the "push" into Germany. Another of her brothers, Elmer, was a member of a reconnaissance unit in Germany. Junior was still in England awaiting orders. He was separated from German- occupied France and Germany itself by only a channel of water. On her world map the space between them was so very small.

The "push" came as a massive shove. It was D-Day, June 6, 1944.

Edward R. Murrow, the news commentator announced, "The largest amphibious assault in the history of war took place today across the English Channel to the shores of France, when hundreds of Allied ships were used to transport the soldiers, vehicles, and supplies that were to invade German held territory. The landing included over 5,000 ships, 11,000 airplanes, and over 150,000 service men.

"After years of meticulous planning and seemingly endless training for the Allied Forces, it all came down to this: The boat ramp goes down, then men jump, swim, run, and crawl any way they can to the cliffs. Many of the first young men entered the surf carrying eighty pounds of equipment. They faced over

200 yards of beach filled with land mines, barricades, barb wire and murderous obstacles before reaching the first natural feature offering any protection. Blanketed by small-arms fire, pinned down by deadly machine gun barrages and bracketed by artillery, they found themselves in living hell."

In spite of heavy American losses, the result was a giant foothold on the mainland of Europe for the Allied forces. Two ports were now opened to the Allies, providing a way for equipment and soldiers to move rapidly into France to back up the original Allied Force. When D-Day was over the Allied Forces had suffered nearly 10,000 casualties; more than 4,000 were dead.

The Germans were now on the defensive, but what about the war in the Pacific? Clara was concerned about the war in Europe because her son and two brothers were there. She was concerned about the war in the Pacific because her son-in-law, Bob, was there. Our armed forces were engaged on battle fronts all over the world.

Japanese began their offensive in China, attacking U.S. air bases in eastern China. The first mission by B-29 super fortress bombers occurred as 77 planes bombed Japanese railway facilities at Bangkok, Thailand. Clara knew her son-in-law was a mechanic working on B-29's in India. She wondered if these B-29's were the very ones he kept repaired.

U.S. Marines invaded Saipan in the Mariana Islands and the first bombing raid on Japan took place as 47 B-29's based in Bengoel, India, targeted the steel works at Yawata. The "Marianas Turkey Shoot" occurred as U.S. carrier-based fighters shot down 220 Japanese planes, while only 20 American planes were lost. Progress was slowly occurring, but it was still a long way to Tokyo.

Like everyone, Clara worried and wondered when the terrible war might end.

Chapter 16

Barefoot Rituals

"Mom, Mom, I got chicken poop between my toes!" Jean came screaming to the screen door of the house. Hobbling on the heels of her bare feet she continued to shriek. "Eeuuuuu, Eeuuuuu, I stepped in chicken poop! It's between my toes, get it off, get it off!"

Stepping in greenish-yellow, sticky and oozing chicken poop was one of summer's hazards of going barefoot on the farm. The chickens on the Bradford farm never could be contained behind the fence of the chicken coop, but had full range of the yard around the house and the barnyard. It was common for one or two to get out in the road, too. When that happened it was one of the younger children's responsibility to shoo them back. Occasional you would hear the honking of a car horn, the squawk of a chicken and look up to see feathers flying everywhere. When that happened the family had meat during the week instead of just on Sunday.

"Go to the well and pump water on it." Clara commanded. "Don't come in the house with that on your foot!"

Jean hopped around to the back of the house and pumped a cold flow of water over her gooey toes. The chicken poop stuck like paste. She pumped again and again to get every bit of it from between her toes. Dancing on one foot she viewed her messy one. Not wanting to touch it, she finally swished it around in a full pail of water until the poop was all gone.

The children loved to go barefoot. As soon as Clara was assured that the frost was out of the ground and the earth had warmed up enough, she gave the long awaited signal that the shoes could be removed. The shoes were flung off and the good earth felt warm and inviting between their toes. The shoes would not go back on again until school started in September, or if they went into town. She had two reasons for doing so. One was to save on their shoes, even though they would probably outgrow them by fall anyway. They were saved because there was always a younger sibling who would grow into them. The other reason was to accommodate the nagging request from the children, which began as soon as the snow melted.

Going barefoot always created a safety problem too. At least one of the children during the summer would step on a protruding nail, often rusty, which would demand immediate attention. Clara should have been a nurse the way she tended to her injured children. A nail-pierced foot was immediately soaked in a dishpan of Epson salts. After thoroughly drying the foot, she dabbed stinging iodine on the wound while the recipient squirmed and begged for mercy.

"It'll only hurt for a minute."

She would then take a worn-out dish towel, which was originally a bleached-out grain bag, tear off several strips and wrap the injured foot in several layers of snow white rags.

Stubbing a toe on a stone, or getting a toe caught in the spokes of the family bicycle were common happenings.

When shoes first came off it took a while for tender feet to toughen up. But by mid- summer the children could run barefoot down the gravel road without feeling any pain.

Saturday when the Bradfords went to town, it was a scramble to find a matching pair of shoes that would fit. They couldn't go to town without shoes. Often their feet would not fit into the shoes they had discarded in the spring. One of the twins could often fit into Alden's shoes, and Alden's feet were large enough to fit in a pair Junior had left behind. Jean could wear one of the twin's and John would wear Bill's, and finally, Bill would often wear a pair of Jean's outgrown shoes. It was a hodgepodge accumulation of footwear. Clara always wanted to be proper and wanted her children to be, also. The children who could not find shoes to fit, in some sort of fashion, simply had to stay home or sit in the car. Clara didn't want it known that they did not have enough money to put shoes on their children's feet. Ration stamps for shoes far outnumbered the amount of money needed to buy them.

It was the summer of 1944 and Junior was now in France driving a 6 X 6 army truck as part of the massive D-Day invasion. He brought supplies to the troops in front lines who were pushing the enemy back toward their homeland of Germany. He could not tell her that in his letters, but she could read between the lines. Clara prayed for his safety. She wished he had nothing more to worry about than shoes that fit or chicken poop between his toes. However, that was doubtful.

Chapter 17

There's a War Going On

"Tonight, as on every other night, the rooftop watchers are peering out across the fantastic forest of London's chimney pots. The anti-aircraft gunners stand ready."

Clara listened to the radio broadcast as Edward R. Murrow reported on the war with strong visual images. Grandma listened from across the room while darning the children's socks.

"I have been walking tonight -- there is a full moon, and the dirty-gray buildings appear white. The stars, the empty windows are hidden. It's a beautiful and lonesome city where men and women and children are trying to snatch a few hours sleep underground."

Hitler gave the order to attack England in June of 1944, shortly after the Allied landings at Normandy, with his newest weapon, the V1 flying bombs or the Buzz Bombs as Londoners called them, It was a unique and deadly weapon, an unmanned flying bomb launched from northern France by catapults but eventually also released from airplanes. It flew at low range over the landscape until it reached its intended target, usually the center of London, where it descended and exploded. In all a total of 9,251 flying bombs were launched. Many were shot down by anti-aircraft gunners, intercepted by RAF fighters or caught in the mooring cables of defense balloons, But still over 2,300 got through to terrorize Londoners and wreak destruction.

Clara's heart ached for the people of England, and especially the children. She was deeply engrossed in the news report when her children came bounding into the house.

"Mom, Mom!" The three younger ones, in chorus, ran into the house with the screen door banging shut behind them. "Can we play in the rain?"

"Oh, sorry, Mom" one of them spoke when realizing their mother was listening to the news. They often got scolded for interrupting her during news time.

Her smile signaled the disturbance was all right.

"Can we p-l-e-a-s-e, Mom?" The youngest begged.

It was a gentle rain without thunder, lightning or wind so the okay was given.

"Thank God for the interruption," Clara muttered to herself. She was thankful for the reprieve from the war. Thank goodness for her innocent children who were safe from war.

The children threw off their clothes down to underwear and dashed out into the warm rain. Clara watched from the window as they spun and twirled with arms outstretched and faces turned up to the heavens. They were uninhibited. Free from clothes and worries. And then they stood still in that position. The healing rain caressed their suntanned faces, formed rivers over bare chests and cascaded down dusty legs and onto bare and mosquito-bitten feet.

As the rain let up, they ran in the new puddles, splashed one another and chased each other around the yard. They slipped and fell in the wet grass and laughed until their sides ached. They floated corn cobs on the new rivers which would be gone tomorrow, threw stones in the puddles to hear the "plunk" and watch the water splash.

They were carefree children, safe from harm, and oblivious to the terrible atrocities of war. There was no need for them to listen for the sound of a Buzz Bomb, or hear the wail of the air-raid siren. They were safe. There was no need for them to run for refuge or to sleep in an underground shelter where they were safe from harm, like the children in London.

That evening Clara was so thankful to read that the Slout Players would be back in town again this year. A diversion from the war was needed. Their big tent would be pitched on the

Mill Street lot as usual, and a complete new show of plays and vaudeville acts would be presented for the entire week, she read in the paper. Five nights packed full of hilarious laughter.

She so longed to go and take the children to at least one performance. She wanted to laugh at their silly antics and remember their humorous jokes. But she knew it was not possible. The cost of forty cents for adults and twenty cents for children was simply out of the question.

She wouldn't even ask Dad because she could just hear him say "Judas Priest, Buster, there's a war going on!" Just the thought of them being in town conjured up times when the world was at peace and the family could go on excursions from time to time. The pleasant memories made her smile.

Chapter 18

Topsy Visits Aunt Eva

Early morning, just as the sun begins to break over the eastern sky, is the best time on the farm. The sights and sounds cannot be duplicated. Clara was up earlier than Dad today. With a cup of fresh coffee in her hand and a sweater over her shoulders she went to the back porch. Sitting on the steps she witnessed the farm coming alive. This was a rare occasion for her. She seldom had time for herself without a demanding chore to do or children to care for. Everyone else was asleep.

The fog was lifting from the swamp to the south. The frogs had stopped their nighttime serenade and it was so very quiet. The steam rose from her cup of coffee and spiraled up and out of sight. She was conscious of her own breathing. Grasping the cup with both hands she inhaled the pleasant coffee aroma. The fresh earth after the cleansing rain was renewed with hope.

In the stillness of the early morning she dreamed of her childhood up north with her parents, brothers and sisters. She, one of the oldest of 17 children, had many memories. Memories of swimming in the cold river, running in the woods, playing games, sitting on the floor around the big fireplace on a chilly evening, eating apples and popcorn, of being a carefree child without grown-up concerns or worries.

She was homesick. Before the war, they went back for a few days each summer. She remembered the last time. The children all pilled in the old car at four in the morning and Dad, in the driver's seat, ate fresh-roasted peanuts from Boices Bazaar and smoked cigars as he drove north. The children had a contest on who could spot the first Burma Shave sign. "Soap May Do," was the first sign and on down the road was another - "For Lads with Fuzz" - and then farther on another read; "But Sir, You Ain't "- - on down the road another- "The Kid You Wuz"- - followed by "Burma Shave." Clara chuckled to herself over the enjoyment the children found in such simple things. It would be almost dark by the time they drove into the homestead yard northeast of Grayling. Her mother, seeing them coming, would run to the car to greet them while drying her hands on the corner of her apron. No matter how homesick she was, with gas rationed and no tires to be bought, the trip home would just have to wait until after the war ended.

The rooster aroused her from her thoughts. He was the first to awaken. He strutted down from his night perch, shook his feathers, stretched his neck and let out a loud "cock-a-doodle-do." In the stillness of the morning it seemed so loud; much louder than necessary. She resented having her thoughts disturbed. The rooster's loud message was a reminder for all farm animals that night had ended and a new day had dawned. In the distance one could hear the neighbor's rooster echo the call.

The hens were first to respond. One by one they hopped off their night perch, fluffed their feathers and went about the yard clucking and scratching in the fresh soil to locate any new insects after yesterday's rain. The rooster crowed again. The cows in the barnyard gently mooed. Lying with their feet comfortably folded beneath them, they were not nearly as concerned about a new day as the rooster. They switched their tails and could almost be heard to say, "Ok, we heard ya! We'll get going in a minute, just give us another few minutes to chew our cuds."

The whinnies of the horses, which stand to sleep, was a more energetic signal that they were, like the rooster, ready to begin the day. Most other farmers had converted to tractor power before the war, but horse power was still used on this farm, assisted by the old truck. There would be no thought of owning a tractor until after the war. For now the horses tilled and planted the ground, cut and raked the hay, cut and bundled the wheat and oats with a binder, and cultivated the field corn and the large family garden. They had hard work to do and while somewhat eager to begin work each morning, they were even more eager to stop at the end of the day.

The birds in the spirea bush flew from their nest and soared into the sky, out and about looking for food. Clara mused over the old saying "the early bird gets the worm!" A crow could be heard in the distance. She wished she were as free as the birds.

In rhythm with nature, all the farm animals were now up, even the pigs in the pen were on their feet rooting about for food. Dad was also up, and after slipping on tattered overalls, was stirring barefoot inside the house.

The peacefulness of the farm nearly overshadowed the dismalness all around. The main barn stood with missing siding and gaping holes exposing the hay in the loft, and the adjacent cow barn prevailed with a sagging roof. The chicken coop with several broken windows and only a suggestion of a fence complemented the pig pen that could only contain the laziest of animals. There was no indication that any of the buildings ever had a coat of paint. Just before dawn and after a fresh snowfall the farm looked its very best; partially hidden by darkness or covered with snow.

Clara rose from the porch, tipped the coffee cup for the last bit of coffee before retreating to the house to officially begin another day. Everyone would soon be awake and ready for breakfast. Today like most would be busy.

"Jean!" she called up the stairs, "Aunt Eva will pick you up sometime this morning. Make sure you put on clean underwear!" Aunt Eva often took Jean home with her for a few days. She called Jean "Topsy" after a character she read about in a book, who was left to raise herself without much guidance. Eva felt that Jean needed to be taken away from all those boys from time to time! Clara didn't seem to mind that Jean could climb trees, swing on the hay rope, spit and bat a ball as good as her brothers, but Eva believed she needed occasional refinement.

Jean loved going there. Uncle Harry spent most of his time in the fields and the barn, so it was mostly just Aunt Eva and Jean. Her house was always clean and neat. The living room was especially pretty, with carpet on the floor, and doilies on the table that held a lamp with a lacy lampshade. The davenport held frilly little pillows, and across the back and on each arm were crocheted doilies. The front porch was a haven. It was all screened-in free from flies and insects. At one end was a swing that could hold two people. It was fastened to the ceiling with long chains. It, too, had a cushion and fancy pillows. Jean could sit and swing forever! At the other end were two easy chairs where Aunt Eva and Uncle Harry sat to read the paper after supper. The porch opened out to a green freshly-cut lawn where a croquet game was usually set up. Sometimes in the evening after the milking was done, Uncle Harry would challenge anyone who was willing to a game.

One of the best parts of the visits would be when Aunt Eva got her old familiar hat box down from the shelf of her closet. "Go wash your hands." she would say, making sure the contents would not become soiled or smudged. Inside the box was a treasure of photographs and tintype pictures of old relatives that Jean had never met but with whom she was fascinated. Also in the box was a bundle of letters tied together with a ribbon.

"OK, Mom. Will I stay overnight?"

"She said she would take you to her house for a day or two".

Jean packed her pajamas, clean underwear and a change of clothes. She remembered a time when she stayed with Aunt Eva and the two of them went to town. It was a Thursday, the day of the community chest drawing on the Island. Jean didn't have a dress to wear to the weekly festivities, and young children simply could not go unless they were properly dressed. So Aunt Eva took her into the Hafners 5 and 10-cent store on the corner of Main and E. Hamlin Street and bought her one. The clerks stood around to shield her from public view, while she slipped off her worn shorts and blouse and put on the brand new beautiful yellow dress with pink flowers. Aunt Eva paid the clerk sixty-five cents.

"Hurry Jean, Aunt Eva is here!" came the call from downstairs.

For the next few days Clara worked in the garden, especially in the cool of the evening. The papers and radio urged people to grow their own food. "Grow a Victory Garden and help win the war!" Growing her family food was nothing new for Clara. She had always grown a garden for as long as she could remember, war or no war.

As she hoed around each plant she hummed to herself the tune she sang so often these days- - "There is work to be done, to be done, There's a war to be won, to be won."

Buccaneer Airplane built by the twins

Chapter 19

The Runaway Buccaneer

She kneaded the bag with vigor. The bag contained the white lard-like substance that held the little yellow "pill" somewhere within. When the pill was broken it spread the color dye and made the oleo yellow. Squeeze and knead, squeeze and knead. The family normally used butter. But butter cost thirty cents a pound, where oleo was only eighteen cents. Even though butter was much preferred, Clara tried from time-to-time to slip the less expensive oleo onto the supper table.

The twins bounded onto the back porch and through the kitchen door. As they frequently did, they were on their way upstairs and to their workbench. They wanted to give their model plane a final inspection before declaring it worthy of flying. They had built planes before, but this was the first one that would fly with an engine in its nose.

"What's that?" Lyle, asked as he passed his Mother.

"It's oleo," Clara answered.

"Why oleo? Why not butter?" he continued in disgust.

"Because it's cheaper and besides you'll never know the difference as soon as I get it mixed. When it's mixed it's yellow just like butter."

She knew her statement about not knowing the difference was not true. Dad knew the difference, Grandma also knew, as well as all the children who could tell the difference between real yellow, creamy butter made at Millers Dairy Farms and "lard", as the twins often called it, that had to be colored.

"Here, give me a hand!" She handed the bag to Lyle.

He shook his head as his twin quickly answered in his place.

"We gotta get her ready, Mom. We're going to fly it after supper if the wind goes down." Kyle was talking about flying the free-flight model plane they completed just last night. Early in the spring Mr. Swan, across the road, took the twins to Lansing to a hobby shop where they selected a Berkley Buccaneer kit with a wingspan of fifty-four inches and a Rogers 29 motor. Mr. Swan paid for most of it. The agreement was that the twins would build the plane and the three of them would fly it together. The twins spent every spare moment cutting the delicate pieces from the sheets of balsa wood, then pinned them to the blueprint, where they were left to dry after gluing. They covered the structure with tissue paper and then sprayed water to tighten the skin and take out all the wrinkles before giving it a final coat of "dope" to strengthen the covering.

After supper and the evening milking were done, the twins took their prized plane across the road where the three of them would launch it on its maiden flight. The gas tank of the two-cycle engine was filled with a mixture of oil and gasoline. The coil and condenser were in place, as were the flashlight batteries.

Kyle adjusted the rudders in such a manner that he hoped it would fly in circles. And Lyle pulled out the air timer that would cut off the engine after a minute and a half. It seemed to be ready.

Mr. Swan spun the propeller and the engine came to life. With the plane held high in his right hand he ran several yards across the open field before it took hold, lifted and left his hand.

The Burkley Buccaneer with its five-foot wing span was launched!

The whole neighborhood turned out for the test flight. With a dozen or so sets of eyes turned toward the setting sun, they watched in amazement as the plane climbed into the cloudless sky with the grace of an eagle.

The twins felt pride as they viewed their graceful accomplishment dip and soar. They were filled with a feeling they could not explain. They wondered if they would ever pilot a real plane someday? Would they ever feel the freedom of a bird? Or, would they be stuck on the farm forever?

It soon became obvious that Kyle's rudder adjustment was not sending the plane in circles, but rather sending it high in the air where it caught the air thermals and glided out of sight.

Mr. Swan immediately jumped on his motorcycle to chase in the last seen direction. One of the boys leaped on behind him while the others got into Mrs. Swan's '36 Ford while she drove in hot pursuit of the runaway plane.

Days later a neighbor stopped at the house to tell the boys the plane had crash- landed in his field. They immediately retrieved it, patched it up and made it ready for another launch.

The twins spent the summer flying and searching the countryside for the Berkley Buccaneer with the five - foot wing span and Rogers 29 engine. Between doing their chores and farm work, flying the plane and getting their cows ready to show at the county fair the first of September, it kept them very busy. They were deeply aware, however, that Alden had joined the Navy, and would be going soon for his physical and induction into the navy.

Chapter 20

The Driving Lesson

"Jean! Jean!" Dad was calling from the kitchen. "Jean, I need ya to drive the truck. Gotta get up some hay this afternoon before it rains."

"Why can't one of the boys do it?" she called back from her bedroom upstairs.

"They got other things to do! Come on, I need ya."

"But Dad, I don't know how to drive!" she reminded him.

"Judas Priest, come on, you can do it! I'll show ya!"

Whether she knew how to drive or not was a minor issue, in Dad's opinion. When he made a request, the children responded without any "back talk" as he called it. The fact that she was eleven years old and short for her age added nothing to his decision. He needed help and these obstacles were only minor to him.

The flatbed truck with the hay loader hooked behind was already in the field. It was hard to walk in the hay stubble barefoot but she didn't want to disappoint her Dad. She walked to the truck, pretending the sharp stubbles that pierced her feet had no effect. Bill and John followed along.

"Now, lets see. Can ya reach the pedals?" Dad stood at the opened driver door and adjusted the coil spring seat as far forward as it would go.

She sat at the very edge of the seat and stretched her legs toward the pedals as far as she could. She could barely reach them. The big black steering wheel seemed huge to her.

He reached across her lap and put the long shifting rod that came out of the center of the floor to "neutral." He then reached down on the floor at her feet, and pushed a small lever to the left of the three pedals. The motor roared to life.

"Now," he shouted his instructions over the noise of the motor. "Now, that's the clutch, that's the brake and over there is the gas." He pointed to the pedals below from left to right.

Jean repeated, "The clutch, brake and gas." trying so hard to remember. She was accustomed to only being told once, as were the other children.

"First ya push down the clutch with your left foot. Then push the shifting gear straight up to creeper. "

She followed instructions.

"No, no! That's second gear! Put it back to neutral and pull it close to ya, as far as it goes, and then push it straight up."

"Okay, good! Now give it a little gas with your right foot and at the same time let out on the clutch real slow. Not now, not now! Judas Priest, I'll tell ya when! Ya think ya got it?"

She shook her head yes.

Dad closed the door.

"Oh, I forgot to tell ya. Keep the truck straddle the windrow." He shouted "When I need ya to stop, I'll pound on the cab of the truck."

With the instructions understood, Dad climbed onto the bed of the truck.

Her younger brothers sat in the seat next to her. They were so excited that their big sister now knew how to drive. They bounced in their seat and looked through the clouded windshield onto the spirals of hay which had been raked into windrows across the entire field.

Dad shouted from the back that he was ready. He would take the hay as it was delivered to the bed of the truck and spread it around evenly.

"Go, go, go!" Bill and John urged in unison.

Jean pushed on the gas pedal until the engine roared even more. She slowly let out on the clutch, just as she had been instructed.

The truck leaped forward. Fearing it was too fast, she pulled her foot off the gas, then realizing it needed some gas, she gave it more. The truck began to leap and bolt like a colt the first time a saddle is slung over its back.

"Judas Priest!" came the shout from the back. "Judas Priest and a whole lot of other words, delivered in a sing-song manner. Words that were never spoken in the house. He had been dropped to the truck bed and was trying to regain his footing and get back on his feet.

By the time the second set of "Judas Priest" and all those other words were delivered, she finally got the "feel" of the power and was able to smooth out the ride.

Bill and John enjoyed the jumpy, bumpy start. They laughed and bounded up and down. Jean did not laugh. Her little hands were sweaty and dirty from tightly grasping the big steering wheel as they crept across the hay field. Her thick black hair felt hot and sweaty. Being shingled up the back gave her some relief, but the bangs across her forehead were wet and clung to her face. They needed to be pushed back, but she couldn't take her hands off the steering wheel to do it.

Through the cracked and clouded windshield Jean saw the end of the field looming ahead. She didn't know how she was supposed to maneuver the big long truck with the hay loader attached. Was she supposed to stop it, or make a long swing and turn it around?

She didn't even know how to stop it. Dad never told her how! Way before it was necessary, she left the windrow and made a large swooping turn to get back straddling the windrow headed in the other direction. In doing so, she left big sections of two windrows, the one she left and the one going the other way. She expected to hear another "Judas Priest" and lots of other words for missing so much hay, but Dad said nothing.

Dad pounded on the cab with his pitchfork to stop. Jean, not knowing what to do, let up on the gas. The truck jerked to a stop, and the motor finally killed.

By the time the hay was all loaded, Jean had learned how to press the gas pedal just so while releasing the clutch. Dad could even stand up when she started up. She learned the other gears too- - creeper, first, second and high. Reverse was more difficult. A silver lever near the knob of the shifting lever had to be raised and the stick shoved way over toward the passenger side before pulling it down.

At the supper table that evening, Dad told what a good job Jean did driving the truck. He never said her jerky starts knocked him down or that she skipped a large portion of the hay when she turned the truck around. He simply told the whole family that she did a good job.

"Much obliged." he nodded in the direction of his young daughter.

Chapter 21

Peaches, Feed Bags & Sheets

"Peaches are plentiful this year and are $1.98 a bushel for Elbertas at the A & P." Clara was relaying the information from the *Eaton Rapids Journal.*

"Oh, Dad, I need at least two bushels." Gathering together four dollars at one time to buy peaches was out of the question. However, one bushel could be purchased.

She continued to read from the paper. The news centered around a new canning center in the High School Home Economics Building under the direction of Mrs. Elna Mattson. "It's open to the public and is available for the use of any family in the community. This is the school's contribution to the war effort."

"Listen to this," she read. "The equipment in the canning center is the most modern and up-to-date, including pressure cookers, gas plates, meat grinders, chopping blocks, can sealers, scalding and blanching baskets. Number two and three cans will be used, and cans may be purchased at cost. A General Electric dehydrator is part of the equipment. If not enough sugar is available, the dehydrator for preservation of food can be used".

Clara continued, "A recent statement from the president of the U.S. states that food preservation is much more necessary now than ever before. Whatever can be raised and preserved will be a big help at home and toward victory."

The Journal reports that "Mrs. Otto Souza was the first to use the canning center when she canned two bushels of peas. She was assisted by her son Dennis and Orman Finch."

"Mrs. Viola Foster and Mr. and Mrs. Lowell Mitchell have established a new record shelling a bushel of peas in one hour. They shelled and canned their peas in two and one-half hours.

"Mrs. Donald Bush canned carrots, Mrs. George Pettit canned green beans and Mrs. D.B. Hargrave processed 30 cans of green and wax beans. Also, Mrs. Warren Hall canned 49 cans, Mrs. Frank Post, 15 cans, Mrs. Dean Winter, 19 cans and Mrs. Harold Field, 35 cans of green beans; Mrs. Herbert VanAken, 40 cans of green and wax beans, Mrs. Groat, 14 cans of currants and Mrs. Wendell Wilbur, 21 cans of pork."

She went on, "However, all previous records were dwarfed when Mrs. Wess DesGranges, a mother of eleven, canned 4 bushels of string beans which equaled 82 number-3 cans and 12 number-2 cans. Later she canned an additional 195 number

3 cans and 42 number-2 cans of beans and 19 number-3 cans of chicken."

Clara believed it would be nice to do her canning in the new canning center with all the up-to-date equipment and running water; water that ran from a spigot at the sink and didn't need to be pumped and carried into the house by the pailful. Even though it was open to the community, she wasn't sure she was entitled to use the facility since all her children, except for the three older ones, now went to Olivet to school. Their mailing address was Eaton Rapids, when they went to town they went to Eaton Rapids, but now the school bus stopped at their door and picked up the children and took them to Olivet to school. It was just as well, she did her canning at home in bits and pieces between getting meals, washing, ironing, cleaning, gardening and tending to the children. She already had dozens and dozens of glass canning jars filled with wax beans, tomatoes, cherries, and would soon have a bushel of peaches in jars, too.

She read where Howard Umbarger was missing in action somewhere in France. Her heart went out to him and his parents. She also read where another local young man, Lt. Glenn Marr, was killed in action somewhere over England. The war news was so dismal.

The allied forces were pushing through France and were near the German border. Japan introduced their first "Kamikaze" or suicide air attacks against the United States warships in Leyte Gulfe in the Philippines. She was later to learn that during the war Japan sent 2,257 Kamikaze pilots in airplanes to crash into Allied ships, with the hopes of destroying them.

Clara just had to put the paper down and get to work. She would make sheets for the beds this afternoon. The old ones were getting so thin and worn, especially on the boys' beds. Grandma had patched them just about as many times as a sheet could be patched. It was time to relegate the old sheets to the rag bag where they would be ripped in strips and used as bandages as needed.

The empty chicken feed bags had been saved all summer, seams taken out, washed and placed flat out in the lawn for the sun to bleach out the printing. They were now neatly folded next to the sewing machine, ready to be sewed together into sheets.

Not all the feed bags were used for sheets, many of them were used as dish towels. Sometimes it took several washings before all the printing came off the bags. It wasn't uncommon to have the faded red emblem of Purina Chicken Feed with the bright sun rays still visible on new sheets and dish towels.

Clara moved the sewing machine out from the wall, opened the lid and pulled up the head of the machine. She hooked the long belt over the drive wheel attached to the foot treadle that made the sewing needle go up and down.

It took four feed bags to make one sheet. They were sewed together making one big square and then hemmed around the four sides.

She spent the afternoon making sheets. The rhythmic clatter of the machine was almost hypnotic. Clara worked the treadle and dreamed of a day when the dinner table would be set for the whole family, when life would be easier, when she could buy new shoes, coats and clothes for the children, when she could go into the grocery store and buy whatever she pleased. She especially dreamed of the day when there would be enough gasoline for a trip up north to visit her folks.

Right now she hoped for the day she could buy regular, snow white, soft cotton sheets; sheets that did not have seams down and across the middle. But then she thought of the G.I's who were in foxholes, lying in mud trying to keep dry and warm, fearing incoming mortar rounds or shells and bombs. What they wouldn't give for one of her handmade sheets. Or the homeless children in London who would welcome a bed of any description where it was safe. She decided that sleeping on sheets with seams down the middle and across the center was a very small discomfort, compared to the sacrifice other people were making. She silently prayed for victory.

WWII poster to encourage the home front to work together for the war effort.

Chapter 22

Chicken Feed Curtains and Dresses

Dad was now bringing home chicken feed from the mill in a new kind of bag.

Long Bean & Grain Company offered their customers a choice of the usual standard white bag or, for ten cents more, the brand new bags made of dress-print fabric.

The printed bags came in colorful flower prints on a white background with several designs to choose from- - each one as beautiful as the other. Dad felt the extra ten cents was well worth it.

He usually took whichever bags were on top and easier to load onto the truck, but when Jean started going with him, she carefully picked out each one. "I'm going dress shopping with Dad!" Jean called to her mother as the truck rolled out of the yard, heading toward Eaton Rapids and the mill.

Once there, she scrutinized the pile of printed bags with chicken feed inside before beginning her selections. No matter how many bags had to be moved to get to the ones of her choice, Dad moved them without too much grumbling.

Occasionally he would say "Judas Priest, Jean, make up your mind. I've got to get home and start the chores." Or "Jean, there are other folks waiting, hurry up."

She chose each one carefully and calculated how many bags of each she needed. Once they were emptied of chicken feed, she would be wearing them either as a skirt or dress. She wanted them to her liking. She chose the ones that were fewer in number so others would not be wearing the same print. It took two to make a broomstick skirt, if you wanted it real full and pretty, and three to make a dress.

Clara transformed the dreary kitchen into a farm wife's dream with the use of the printed bags. She went at it with gusto. Adding prettiness to one's surroundings was very uplifting during the war years. When the newspapers and news broadcasts painted such a dreary picture of the war and destruction, a bit of beauty in the home was indeed very refreshing.

After the bags were emptied, if the correct thread was pulled, the stitches would come out in a minute making it into a single length of fabric. However, finding the correct thread was not always easy. With the bags opened, laundered, dried and pressed they were ready to be made into any creation of your choosing.

Clara purchased a package of Rit dye in a lovely shade of green that matched the leaves of the flowers in the feed bags she had been saving. Following the directions on the package she dyed several of the plain white bags.

Placing the large copper boiler on the kitchen range, she filled it with water from the pump outside. Bucket after bucket was carried in and dumped in the boiler. A few more sticks of wood were added to the fire. In a few hours the water was steaming hot. The contents of the dye package were added to the hot water and, with the use of a broken broom handle, the water was swished back and forth until the dye was completely dissolved. Each white feed bag was unfolded and placed in the green water. With the use of the same broom handle, the bags were stirred, trounced and agitated until she was sure the dye was evenly distributed.

"Ain't that enough?" one of the children asked.

"Isn't that enough?" Clara corrected.

"That's what I said, isn't that enough?"

"I want to make sure the dye has taken." Clara smiled.

She pulled one piece after another out of the steaming water for closer inspection. After she was satisfied, the job of rinsing them in cold water began. Finally the wet bags were pinned to the clothesline to dry.

It wasn't until the next day that the transformation began. The top of the sewing machine was unloaded, the head pulled up, the belt put in place and new oil was squirted into the oil holes. With a tape measure around her neck, scissors in her apron pocket, a string of safety pins fastened to the yoke of her apron, a stack of solid green bags and another stack of printed bags, she was ready to begin.

After she inserted the bobbin and threaded the needle, she pumped the sewing machine, sewed in smooth even stitches, tied knots in the end threads, cut and pressed the curtains. Finally she nailed curtain rods in place.

Curtains over the top of the short sink window were first to be made. They were made entirely of the printed fabric. When strung onto the curtain rod they ruffled in crisp, clean beauty. The sink below was encircled with the solid green fabric, with a ruffle at the bottom made from the matching print. Across the room near the table was a full-length double window. Across the very top a ruffle was made of print, to match the one over the sink. In the center of the window a curtain of solid green, with matching print on the bottom edge, covered the lower half of the two windows.

Over the window in the door that opened onto the back porch, a simple printed ruffle was placed at the very top. The kitchen was beautiful! She felt better, too. Life didn't seem as drab as it was just that very morning.

She would later carry her enthusiasm to feminize Jean's bedroom and even her own, adding new beauty to the dreary rooms.

Not only were home decorations made, but garments of every description were sewn together. Dresses, skirts, shorts, halter tops, bathing suits, jackets, pajamas and aprons were a few of the items made at the Bradford household using feed bags.

The printed feed bags brought new life to many farm homes. In a world of war, rationing, shortages, loneliness and want, the dress-print feed bags brought beauty, loveliness and renewal to the home front.

Winona brings the "City" to the farm on her weekend visits. She is disappointed there is no letters today. Mail, especially during WWII, was the only means to keep in contact with loved ones.

Chapter 23

Winona's Visit

Winona was home for the weekend. The family was always excited to have her home. She came as often as possible. Sometimes she rode with her cousin Verna when she visited her parents. She and her husband and children also lived in Battle Creek . Other times she took the bus and was picked up at the bus depot in Charlotte.

The family was eager to hear the news about her job, about her latest letter from Bob and what was happening in Battle Creek. She smelled so good and her hair was combed in the latest style. It was like being connected to the big refined world outside when she came home; a world with running water, inside toilets, big bathtubs, sidewalks, gas cooking stoves, iceboxes in which a chunk of ice was placed regularly, big furnaces in the basement for heat, and dozens of stores and several movie theaters within walking distance. Her world stood in stark contrast to the life of her family on the farm.

Even so, she was eager to come home. She helped around the house, assisted with the cooking and participated in any other project that might be taking place. She took the younger ones for walks in the woods. Down the lane they followed the paths worn deep in the earth by the cattle walking in single file, back and forth, to and from the barn to the pasture, into the woods. In springtime they gathered wildflowers, in the summer they picked Queen Ann's lace from the fencerows and in the fall they gathered hickory nuts along the roadside.

The boys saved their best joke for her homecoming. She always laughed no matter how lame the joke might be.

"Hey Nonna," Bill said. "Mrs. Skunk had two babies named In and Out. How did she tell them apart?"

"I don't know, Billy. How did she tell them apart?"

"In-stink!" He squealed with laughter. Winona laughed and pretended it was the funniest joke she had ever heard.

The Indianapolis 500 race was not held again this year, nor would it be for the duration of the war. The U.S. Open Golf was likewise postponed until the end of the war. But baseball was considered patriotic and the St. Louis Cardinals won the World Series. At home the Eaton Rapids Football team won their opening game 14-2 against Everett from Lansing, in a major upset.

Food rationing continued. It was difficult to obtain replacement parts for automobiles and farm machinery. Thank goodness for baling wire which Dad used to cobble up broken machines to keep them working. Alden used to keep the machinery in repair using the same wire. There were no new tires for the automobile, and taking any kind of a lengthy trip more than ten miles away from home was out of the question. Clara so wanted to go home to the serenity of the north woods where she grew up. She longed to visit her mother and father, if only for a few days. The north held a healing power. It was a place of peace where the air seemed so clear and easy to breathe. A good deep breath could clear the mind and release the stored-up tension. Just to sit around the big dinner table and be pampered by her mother would be so healing. But for now, letter writing would have to do. Maybe next year she could go home.

The War Fund quotas were set for Eaton County for the next two weeks. Eaton Rapids' quota was $2,295 in new war bonds and stamps. Clara wished she could help. Horner's Mill was practically begging for people to come to work. "Farmers and Farmerettes! Now that the crops are nearly in why not come in and see us about an essential war job for the winter months?" That's how Clara got to Eaton Rapids in the first place. Back in 1918 she read a similar ad in the Grayling paper, nearly two hundreds miles away, only it was a different war then.

Winona complained to her mother that her new underpants were held up with a button rather than a rubber elastic band. All rubber was now used for the war effort. "Mom, do you know what happened?" she began. "A friend of mine lost her panties right in the middle of a busy street when the button popped. They fell right down to the ground!" she exclaimed. After that, Winona reinforced her button with a safety pin. She wasn't taking any chances; she could not survive such an embarrassment.

When she was home for the weekend, Saturday night was spent listening to the Lucky Strike Cigarettes Hit Parade rather than the Grand Ole Opry. She, unlike the rest of the family, didn't like country music.

The ten most popular songs of the week were played in reverse order so the number one song was played at the end of the broadcast. She listened faithfully and wrote each song down to send to Bob.

The number one most popular song of the day was "I'll Be Seeing You." It held the first place for twenty-four weeks. Other popular songs were, "Swinging on a Star," "Sentimental Journey," "Ac-cent-chu-ate the Positive," "Long Ago and Far Away," and "Don't Fence Me in." She sang along with the singers and seemed to know all the words. Trying to teach the others the words so they could sing along too, was more difficult.

"Come on kids! Sing with me - - -

You've got to ac-cent-chu-ate the positive

E-lim-i-nate the negative

Latch on to the affirmative

And don't mess with Mr. in between," she urged.

The house seemed so empty after she left on Sunday evening. It was like there had been a death in the family. Junior was away. Alden would soon leave for the navy. Winona went back to her apartment in Battle Creek to start another work week, alone. On the happy side, she would be back real soon. She promised to take Jean back with her for a week yet this summer. Maybe she would be back as soon as next weekend!

The shrinking Bradford family gathered around the kitchen table for the usual Sunday evening supper of bread and milk. The children were always high-spirited and full of fun. They were Clara's pride. She laughed at their silliness and silently prayed for their safety. Afterwards, while the others prepared for bed, Clara took out her tablet of writing paper and commenced to write her weekly letter to her boy.

Twelve-year-old Jean in pinafore dress made from feed bags visit a park in Battle Creek. Big sister, Winona, curled Jean's hair.

Chapter 24

Visit to Battle Creek

Clara helped Jean pack a bag with a week's supply of clothes. She wore a brand new pinafore made from feed bags. The blue flower print ruffles fell over her tanned shoulders and the full gathered skirt cinched her small waist and flowed out to her knees. She felt beautiful in this dress. When she twirled, the skirt fanned out, exposing her slip beneath. In the bag were new shorts made from matching fabric and a broomstick skirt and draw string blouse made from yellow flower print feed bags. Also included was a pair of pajamas made from white feed bags.

"Now you be careful and mind Winona," Clara instructed her twelve-year-old daughter. "You'll be gone for a week. Here is some change in case you need it."

"She won't need any money, Mom," Winona interrupted.

The two boarded the Greyhound bus in Charlotte heading to Battle Creek and points beyond. Upon arrival in Battle Creek they walked to Winona's apartment at 25 Bowen Avenue.

The streets were crowded with soldiers in their khaki summer uniforms. Jean had never seen so many. Fort Custer was situated on the outskirts of town, so soldiers milling about was not an uncommon sight for Winona.

"Don't look at them. Just look down. Don't pay any attention to them." Winona instructed her younger sister as they maneuvered through several groups of uniformed men on the sidewalk.

"Hubba hubba hubba!" shouted one.

"Oh you beautiful doll, what is you name?" called another.

"Come to me baby!"

"Cut off my legs and call me shorty!" This was followed by whistles and more hubba, hubba's and wolf calls.

The two looked only at the sidewalk and walked through groups of young men who were out for a Sunday afternoon in town. Jean felt proud that the men found her sister attractive. Winona was indeed a very pretty woman.

Their walk home took them past Percy Jones Hospital. The fenced front yard held wounded soldiers in bandages, on crutches and in wheelchairs. Some had limbs missing. This was Jean's first experience of seeing the results of war. The nurses dressed in sterile white uniforms, with perky little caps on their heads, worked among the men administering comfort. The 1500 bed hospital was the largest U.S. Army medical center. They specialized in neurosurgery, amputations and handicapped rehabilitation, deep x-ray therapy and plastic artificial eyes. In one month alone 729 operations were performed.

Men with large POWs painted on the back of their khaki shirts were mowing the lawn and weeding the flower gardens.

"POW means Prisoner of War." Winona explained. "They were taken prisoners by the Allies and brought here to work. They will go back to Germany when the war is over."

Even though she knew it was impolite, Jean couldn't help but stare. They looked like the young soldiers whom they had just met on the street. She wondered if they had killed any Americans, or if they harbored hate in their hearts. They looked so ordinary. Jean remembered her folks talking about a local Eaton Rapids boy who was a prisoner of the Germans. She wondered if he was as well clothed and fed as these prisoners seemed to be. Somehow she didn't think so.

They climbed the stairs to the second floor apartment. It seemed so warm. Winona quickly opened the windows and a breeze filtered through the spacious living quarters which included a screened-in front porch.

It was almost dark now and the next day was Monday and a work day for Winona. She took a bath and prepared for bed.

Jean put on her freshly laundered pajamas and crawled between the clean seamless sheets of her sister's bed. Winona sat at her dressing table applying nightly crushed cucumber cleansing cream to her face. Jean fell asleep to the aroma of fresh green cucumbers and dreamed she was back home on the farm.

She awoke in the morning to her sister getting dressed for work. From a bottle she rubbed a burnt orange liquid over her legs from above her knees to her toes. She poured a pool in her hand and rubbed, taking long strokes to avoid as many streaks as possible. Jean was awed at such goings on. "We can't get silk stockings." Winona explained.

She slipped into her size nine dress and into her white pumps. She looked at her legs to give them a final inspection to make sure her "hose were on straight" before giving her long auburn hair a final combing. She was indeed beautiful.

Before Winona left for work that morning, she placed a rather large, square card in the front window that had 25, 50, 75 or 100 on separate sides of the card. The number that was placed at the top of the card indicated to the iceman as he drove by, how much ice you wanted placed in your icebox; either 25, 50, 75 or 100 pounds. Winona placed 50 at the top of the card.

There were no icemen in the country so having a man walk into the house with a big chunk of ice in his heavy iron tongs was a new experience. No words were exchanged. He merely slipped the chunk in the top of the icebox and left. Jean gently pulled the long water tray from the bottom of the box being very careful not to spill its contents and dumped it into the sink, as Winona asked her to do. The "icebox" on the farm was a tin bucket that was lowered into the well pit by a rope tied to the handle. Usually only butter was kept in the "icebox" during the extreme heat of summer.

Jean had the run of the apartment during the day. The phonograph and stacks of records were there to be played. She played the hits of the day over and over. "Don't Fence Me In", "Swinging on a Star", "Mairzy Doats", "Dance With A Dolly," and Bing Crosby's "Pistol Packin' Mama", were favorites. "Star Dust" was her least favorite, but she soon learned it was Bob and Winona's "song". She was asked to pick up the morning and afternoon mail from the box downstairs. There was usually a letter from Bob in one or the other mail deliveries.

In the afternoon, Jean put on her new pinafore dress and walked past Percy Jones on her way to town. She couldn't walk by without staring. What a heartfelt adventure for a young country girl. Viewing the wounded made the war very real. It wasn't just something that was listened to over the radio each evening, or read about in the newspaper. It really was happening and here were the men who were there. She wondered how many other men were inside the large fourteen-story hospital building who were too wounded to sit out on the manicured lawn.

The sidewalks in Battle Creek were all cement. She thought about how easy it would be to ride the family bike on a smooth cement surface instead of a gravel road. The soldiers, who were plentiful in the business section, paid no attention to her. She glanced at her reflection in the store windows as she passed. She picked up her step. The department stores were filled with dresses and sportswear in beautiful pastels made from smooth, soft fabric. For the first time her feed bag dress seemed inferior. The theater marquees boasted of the latest movies - -Bing Crosby in "Going My Way" on one and Ingrid Bergman in "Gaslight" on another. Winona had promised they would go to a movie.

The dime store was her favorite place to look. Woolworth's and Kresge's had colorful toys Bill and John would love, new aprons for Mom and Grandma, new shiny pails for Dad and model airplane kits just perfect for the twins. Jean pretended she purchased each one a gift to take home. Having no money made it only a dream. A lunch counter along one side reminded her of supper time, called dinner in the city, and that she should walk back to the apartment to be there when Winona got home from work.

The evenings were so much fun. A picnic on the front porch, a bus trip to Goquac Lake to swim and lie in the sun, or a trip to the Chinese restaurant on the second floor of one of the downtown stores was a real special treat. And going to the movies was the most fun. Each day was a new adventure.

For one week Jean lived in a different world of cement sidewalks, wearing shoes, eating in restaurants, water at the turn of a valve, inside toilets, visiting parks with lovely flowers and walking almost everywhere one desired. No matter how clean and sterile this world was, there was still the reminder of the horror of war, with all of its suffering and despair.

Jean thoroughly enjoyed the week with her sister, and it turned out to be a yearly event as long as the war was on. She was eager to go and just as eager to get back home. She was surprised to know that during her short week away, John had learned to read. He hadn't started school yet. Surely it must be from memory as Grandma read to him each evening, is what the family thought. But when he picked up an unread book and commenced to read, they were convinced that he, indeed, could read.

She was home. Home to where a week of changes were caught up on. Home where red, juicy, tomatoes grew abundantly on the vines in the garden, where she could dig her bare toes into the cool earth, and where the nights were so clear and every star shone as if it had just been polished. Home to where her bed sheets had a seam down the center and across the middle, home to where the family seemed to be glad she was there and where the twins called her "Eleanor." Eleanor after Eleanor Roosevelt, the President's wife, who traveled around the country a lot. "Well, Eleanor, welcome home!" they teased.

She was home but the image of the wounded at Percy Jones stayed vivid in her memory. Whenever the war was discussed around the supper table, the severely injured and limbless American soldiers and the POW's working behind the fenced area remained an unforgettable image.

Ike and Mike they look alike. Which one of ya's is the toughest?

Kyle and Lyle Bradford

Chapter 25

4-H Cows and The County Fair

It's funny how identical twins look exactly alike to others, but look nothing alike to their family.

Complete strangers would stop Kyle and Lyle on the street "Ike and Mike they look alike. Which one of ya's is the toughest"? Over time they learned to simply point at each other and laugh as though it was the first time they had heard the little rhyme.

When they were in first grade in country school, the teacher was so pleased when they came to school one morning and Kyle was missing his front baby tooth. "At last, I can tell you apart!" she exclaimed. That same day when they came back to school after lunch, lo and behold, Lyle's identical tooth was missing. The teacher was able to tell them apart for only one-half a day.

"How ever do you tell them apart?" people would ask in amazement. "Do you ever get them mixed up?"

The answer from a family member was always "No." To the family the boys were as different as night and day. Although they were the same height, same build and had the same black wavy hair, their identical smiles exposed perfect teeth and were so broad their eyes would close. They were identified by their manner and personality and tone of voice- - not by their physical looks. Kyle's personality was easygoing, thoughtful and his smile more spontaneous. Lyle was more direct and eager to take a chance. Kyle was more cautious and a bit more reserved. Their personalities stabilized each other. Lyle would say "Do it!" Kyle would say "Think about it first!"

They were giving their 4H cows their final grooming before being trailered to the fairgrounds in Charlotte, where the cows and the twins would spend a week. They had worked with the Holstein heifers all summer, teaching them to accept a halter, lead, and stand, and not be skittish around people. The black and white heifers looked identical, too, but had different personalities.

In spite of the War, the fair still went on as usual, but without expanding its programs. Throughout the country, 4-H Clubs followed the slogan "Food for Freedom." At the beginning of the war, 4-H established seven national war goals. Three of the goals dealt directly with the need to produce more food and other products for the war effort. Other goals, however, were aimed at helping young people define their citizenship responsibilities in the community.

Nationally the 4-H'ers recorded impressive increases in levels of agricultural production from the previous year. They were directly responsible for over 77,000 head of dairy cattle, 246,000 swine, and 210,000 head of other livestock. 4-H contributed over 40,000 tons of forage crops and 109,000 bushels of root crops. 4-H members produced enough to keep thousands and thousands of soldiers supplied with food and clothing.

Many other activities were canceled during the duration of the war. However, the fair was not. In fact, membership in the 4-H program increased considerably during the war years.

"We gotta make signs with their names on it." Kyle was reminding his twin that an identifying sign was required to be placed above the stanchion in the 4-H barn.

During the sign making, they wished they had given their cows simpler names, like Bess, Bossie or Elsie. But Kyle named his cow Rosie O'Gradie and Lyle named his Bess- A -Mae - Mooch-O, after a popular song of the day.

The next day was Sunday and Dad helped to load the two cows into the back of the truck. They would take the cows and the boys to the fairgrounds and get settled in before the opening of the fair Monday morning.

"Now, do you have everything you need?" Clara was checking with them before they left.

"I've got my toothbrush, a towel and washcloth, soap, along with a blanket.. . . and we got all our stuff for the cows," they said as one. The blanket was to lay over the straw in the corner of the big barn where they would sleep, along with the other boys from around the county showing their summer livestock projects.

"Now, here are some sandwiches and a bag of cookies. I'll bring you clean clothes and more food before the judging." Clara was giving her boys their final instructions. "Oh, and do you have your dollar?"

Their lunch was wrapped in newspaper and tied with a string. They each had a dollar in their pocket to spend for food or on the midway, when they left for their week's stay at the fair.

The fair was the most exciting event of the year, especially for farm children who did not have the opportunity to leave the farm often. The sounds, smells and excitement were alluring. Many children could not sleep the night before, anticipating the excitement of the fair.

The fair opened Monday morning and a flow of spectators walked through the cattle barns, chicken and rabbit displays, sheep and pig barns and the horse barns. The buildings were clustered together at one end of the fairgrounds and near the race track. The boys brushed their cows and polished their horns each day. They kept busy because the cows had to be watered and fed twice daily. To keep them clean, the manure had to be constantly removed and the bedding replaced with fresh straw. Official judging would come on Wednesday. They led the cows daily around and through the tree-shaded grounds between and behind the barns to get them used to the sights, sounds and noise of the fair. At first the cows balked and tried to go in opposite directions, and sometimes tried to break away.

At the opposite end of the fairgrounds was the midway. The smells of hot dogs, elephant ears and cotton candy engulfed the entire fairgrounds. For farm boys the aroma was overwhelming and left hunger pangs even in a full stomach.

The "oomp-pa-pa, oomp-pa-pa" of the merry-go-round could be heard in the distance. The ferris wheel could be seen spinning with swinging seats, going way up in the air and then down again. The laughter and screams from those being twirled on the tilt-a-whirl was compelling. The chants of the vendors- - - "Three chances for ten-cents, two nickels or one thin dime!" "A prize every time!" "Come here, tough guy--

swing the mallet and make the bell ring!" "Tell your fortune for a dime!" "See the bearded Lady!" - - echoed in the air.

Lyle, being Lyle, wanted to go immediately to the midway. "Come on! Let's go! Let's go!" The sounds beckoned him.

Kyle, being Kyle, insisted that they wait until the next day. Kyle was afraid Lyle would spend his whole dollar the first day!

Mom and Dad came on Tuesday, the day before the cows would be judged. She brought more sandwiches and fresh tomatoes from the garden. She made potato salad, and baked two apple pies from the early Transparent tree near the chicken coop. Apple pie was Kyle's favorite. The young ones came. too. Mom spread a blanket on the ground across from the barns and next to the race track for their picnic.

After lunch, Dad rummaged through his pockets and picked out a quarter between the nails, matches, bits of straw, and other sundry stuff, for Jean to spend as she wished on the midway.

Dad left the picnic dinner to get nearer the grandstand to watch the horse pulling contest and later to observe the sulky race with fast-stepping, trotting horses. There was no money for admission to the grandstand where a better view of the events could be seen. Before the war there was always a display of the new farm machinery behind the grandstand. Now that all manufacturing was geared toward the war effort, there was no new farm machinery to view. There were, however, samples of farm crops on display. Corn with stalks seven feet tall, grain, and sugar beets were the ones he was especially interested in.

With each of their hands in hers, Mom walked John and Bill to the edge of the midway where the little cars went round and round on a platform near the merry-go-round. They were given a choice of which to ride. They both chose the little cars. One behind the other, they steered around the track as if they had control over the stationary cars securely fastened to the moving platform. They eagerly waved at their mother each time they passed. Clara was pleased she found enough ticket money in her purse for them to have such enjoyment.

She took them into the floral hall where beautiful flowers were on display, all grown by young 4-H members from the county. The flowers seemed even more lovely and colorful than before, perhaps they reminded her that there was still beauty in this war-torn world. The building exhibiting the sewing, canning and food preparation and garden produce was always of interest to her. She was amazed at the capabilities these young girls exhibited, especially the blue ribbon winners. "They will make good wives one day." she thought to herself.

The afternoon went by quickly. Before leaving for home to tend to the evening chores, Dad searched around in his pockets for more change to leave with the twins.

"We will be back on Thursday, " Clara assured them. "I'll have your clothes washed, and bring more food."

She paused before getting into the car "Oh, lots of luck on the judging tomorrow!"

"Bring another apple pie!" Kyle called to the moving automobile.

Wednesday morning the boys slicked up their cows with a special oil to make their coats glisten. They sprayed them with fly spray and polished their horns before leading them out into the judging ring.

Rosie O'Gradie and Bess -A- Mae Mooch-O behaved themselves quite well as Kyle and Lyle led their summer's work around and around the ring. They stopped to pose them in front of the judges stand each time around. The judges' looked, felt, asked the boys questions, and wrote things on their tablets. The boys' showmanship was also being judged, along with the cows' behavior and their dairy qualities according to breed standards.

After the judging was over Lyle's Bess-A-Mae-Mooch-O was awarded a blue ribbon. Surprisingly, Kyle's Rosie O'Gradie received no ribbons and no awards.

Kyle was disappointed, but instead of being envious he was as happy over Lyle's first place award as Lyle was. There was no sibling rivalry between the twins. After all, these twins were identical.

Bradford kids say good-by to Alden

before he leaves for the Navy

Chapter 26

The Second Blue Star

"Mom, Mom, he's going to shoot me! He thinks I'm a Jap! He's going to shoot me!" Four-year-old John burst into the house and into his mother's arms. "I told him, I ain't no Jap!"

"Johnny, Johnny, Johnny, calm down and tell me what happened."

"He's going to shoot me, Mom," he said between sobs.

"No one is going to shoot you," Clara assured him. "Now tell me what happened."

He finally composed himself enough to say, "Well, I went trick or treat'n with the other kids, and I wore the mask the twins made with the big long funny nose."

"Yes, yes." She saw him leave the house, she knew about the mask. "Go on."

"And, and, we knocked on the door and said 'trick or treat'. And he went for his gun!"

"Oh, Johnny, Mr. Swan wouldn't shoot you!" Clara reasoned.

"He told his mother he was going to get his gun cause there was a Jap at the door. I heard him say it, Mom. He said he was going to shoot the little Jap with the long nose!"

Clara was beginning to see the humor in the incident. Mr. Swan to the north loved to banter and tease the children. He was also the local air raid warden. He drove up and down the road to make sure all the neighbors' lights were off, or shades pulled, during all practice air raid alerts.

"Mr. Swan would never harm you. He was just playing," she consoled her youngest. "And that lady is his wife, not his mother," Clara corrected.

By this time six-year-old Bill was home. He verified the incident but also added, "As soon as Johnny took off running for home Mr. Swan laughed and laughed. Here, Johnny, is some candy he gave us. I already ate mine."

John finally accepted the "joke", but he was cautious for a long, long time.

Clara had not realized what an effect the war news had on the young ones. She would take extra precautions to keep the dreadful news from them and do what she could to make them feel safer.

It was Halloween. Not much usually happened in the country on that evening. The Lions club was holding a big party for the children in the city, complete with bonfire, donuts, cider and a snake dance. However, activity was very limited in the rural area. Dad would tell tales of tipping over outdoor toilets and putting the neighbor's corn binder on the roof of the granary, when he was a boy. Somehow, the children believed the stories got a bit exaggerated over the years.

Alden and the twins had gone in to town and to the movie. After Jean pleaded and begged, at the last minute they finally consented to let her go, too. She was such a nuisance. The boys could seldom get away without her. She threatened at the top of her lungs to "hate them for the rest of her life," if they would not take her.

This would be Alden's last movie before he left for the navy. Winona would be home for the weekend and the Thuma family would be over for Sunday dinner as a farewell gathering before he left.

There would be no wristwatch for Alden as there was for Junior. There simply was not enough money for such luxuries. Alden realized that the war had taken its toll in the past year since Junior had left. He knew there was hardly enough money for the essentials, let alone something as frivolous as a wristwatch. He wasn't expecting anything; he understood.

Unlike Junior's departure on the train, Alden was put on a bus to Detroit. His Mom and Dad drove him to Charlotte to the bus station where they said goodbye.

"I'll write as often as I can, Mom!" he called over the small crowd gathered there.

She could not speak. She tried to fight back the tears as she waved her white hankie at the departing bus.

After induction, Alden was taken by train to Great Lakes Navy Training base in Illinois, near Chicago.

As soon as Clara could get to town she would buy a new flag for the window. She would take down the present one-star flag and replace it with a new two-star flag.

The State Journal reported that the first balloon bomb launched against the United States from Tokyo reached the U.S.A. and killed six people near Lakeview in Oregon. President Roosevelt was elected for a fourth term and the total U.S. war casualties had now passed 500,000.

There were also reports that the German army was stringing wire across the roads and decapitating American soldiers as they drove their trucks and other war machines on their roadways. Junior was a truck driver in Germany. Clara would be especially careful not to talk about these events where the children could hear.

Some good news was that the Umbarger boy was no longer missing in action but now listed as a prisoner of war somewhere in Germany.

Chapter 27

Popcorn and The Grand Old Opry

The fall of the year passed all too quickly. The colored leaves had been everywhere! The red leaves on the hard maples were especially brilliant. One could not help but be awed at Mother Nature's splendor. It was like she waited until just before the first frost to burst forth with every last bit of beauty she possessed. The panoramic view of the magnificent countryside left one flabbergasted with the array of colors. The reds, rusts, oranges and yellows were brilliant in the sunshine.

The walnuts fell from the tree in the front yard at the first frost and were now gathered and placed in the driveway. Hickory nuts were gathered from the only hickory tree on the farm, which stood in the lane. Cracking and removing the nuts was the childrens' task while sitting around the kitchen range on a cool fall evening.

It was Saturday night. Grandma wiped the dishpan extra dry after the dishes were done. The dishpan was now ready for popcorn. And Clara would cut the boys' hair tonight, before the Grand Ole Opry came on the radio.

She unrolled the blue and white striped shoulder apron, which covered the whole person, from around the hair clippers, barber comb and scissors. The stool was set in the center of the kitchen floor and the boys took turns. Since the twins were still in the barn doing the milking, John was first. He wasn't as particular as the older boys, so cutting his hair didn't take nearly as long. Clara spread the large apron around his neck and pinned it tight. His dark thick hair grew unusually fast. Even though she tried really hard to keep the cut hair from going down his neck, it seems some always did, causing itching and irritation.

Clara was certainly experienced in hair cutting. She worked her hand clippers nearly as fast as electric ones. She had cut Dad's hair since they were married, Junior never had an outside haircut until he was drafted, nor did Alden. The twins had, likewise, set on her stool with the apron pinned around their neck since they were toddlers and the same was true of Bill and John. Jean complained that her mom cut so many boys' heads of hair that she didn't know how to cut a girl's hair. So, that is why her hair usually looked so much like a boy's cut, too. Her thick, black hair was cut straight across so her ear lobes showed, and then shingled up the back, just like the boys. Just recently Clara started to let Jean's hair grow longer and even, at times, tried to roll it on rags and make it curl.

Grandma stoked up the fire in the cooking range. The fire had to be hot to make good popcorn. She put bacon grease in the bottom of the big black iron spider and spread kernels of popcorn over the bottom. Covering the spider with a lid she then commenced to move it back and forth, back and forth, back and forth while the kernels exploded within.

The delightful aroma spread throughout the house. The dishpan was full by the time the family gathered around the radio and prepared to listen to the Grand Ole Opry, or the Barn Dance as some called it.

The Barn Dance was preceded by a broadcast of "long haired", as country folks called it, Music Appreciation Hour, conducted by Dr. Walter Damrosch. Afterward, the solemn Old Judge, George D. Hay came on the air saying: "For the past hour, you have been listening to Grand Opera. Now we will present to you the Grand Ole Opry!" Good ole hillbilly music followed.

The family all settled in chairs around the radio. The dishpan of popcorn was passed from one to another.

"First," the Judge said, "we're gonna hear from Roy Acuff and his Smoky Mountain Boys. Smoke it up, Roy."

"From the great Atlantic Ocean to the wide Pacific shore,

From the queen of flowing mountains to the south bells by the shore,

She's mighty tall and handsome and known quite well by all;

She's the combination on the Wabash Cannonball. - - - - -"

It was followed by the comedy of the Duke of Paducah, who finished his segment with "I'm goin' back to the wagon, these shoes are killing me."

There was Uncle Jimmy Thompson who could "fiddle the bugs off a tater vine" and Uncle Dave Macon on his banjo, "It ain't goin' to rain no more!" There was Kitty Wells, the Queen of Country Music. The Tennessee Plow boy, Eddy Arnold, Ernest Tubbs, Cowboy Copas, Lester Flatt and Earl Scruggs added to the musical enjoyment.

Grandpa Jones' fingers flew over his banjo. Hank Williams crooned "The Cattle Call" and "Love Sick Blues. " Little Jimmy Dickens, Mother Maybelle and the Carter Sisters added their special blend of music.

Clara looked up from her mending to see her family around the radio. How peaceful and happy they were. The radio, with a big green tuning eye in the center, sat on a small table in the living room. Dad, like the children, delighted in the music and comedy of the Grand Ole Opry. Their feet kept time to the music and they laughed fully at the antics of Minnie Pearl with her big "HowDeeeee. I am just so proud to be here!" and String Bean, who they imagined was very tall and skinny. Clara savored the moment.

The dishpan of popcorn was empty. The end of the Grand Ole Opry followed when the solemn Old Judge closed by saying:

"That's all for now friends,
Because the tall pines pine,
And the pawpaws pause,
And the bumblebee bumble all around.
The grasshoppers hop,
And the eavesdroppers drop,
While, gently, the ole cow slips away...
This is George D. Hay saying so long for now."

WWII Poster. Women were asked to go to work, too.

Chapter 28

Getting Ready for Winter

It was November, 1944 and the war raged on. In the English Channel, the allied troop carrier, S.S. Leopoldville and all their equipment sank with the loss of 763 men of the US 66th Infantry Division.

On the home front, Roosevelt was elected to his fourth term as President of the United States. The *Eaton Rapids Journal* supported Dewey, as did the Bradfords. Even though they were disappointed they felt Roosevelt should finish the war and bring our country to victory. In that respect, they were not too unhappy with the election.

At home the Horners Woolen Mills were advertising for help. They pleaded for mothers to come to work on the night shift after the children were put to bed. They asked farmers to work for them after the fall harvest was in. Horners were desperate for help to fill their huge government contracts for blankets.

More and more blue stars were going up in windows all around Eaton Rapids as well as the rest of the nation, as young men were being drafted into the service. From time to time a gold star would replace one of blue. The hired man who worked for the Swans to the north was one of the first in the neighborhood to replace the blue star with gold in his trailer window.

At the Bradford house, letters came frequently from both Junior and Alden, as did small government allotment checks, to help compensate for the support the boys would have given the family had they been home.

Even with part of the family missing, life went on with the remaining five children going to school each day. Only now they had to walk to the corner to catch the school bus, rather than it stopping in front of the house. This was to save gas for the war effort. Grandma helped with the daily housework during the day and read to the children at night. Dad worked even longer hours now with the livestock and barn work without the help of the older boys, and Winona came home two or three times each month.

Clara continued with her daily routine, only added to it was constant letter writing. She wrote twice a week to her boys, once a week to Winona and often to her mother and father in Grayling, and occasionally to her three brothers who were stationed in other parts of the world. She helped the children with school work as best her eighth grade education would allow. She was, however, very good at spelling. She could spell any word and it became easy for the children to ask for her help rather than looking up a word in the dictionary. "You really should look it up. You'll remember it if you do," she kept reminding them.

"How can I look it up in the dictionary if I don't know how to spell it?" was their standard answer.

She only smiled and never insisted. She rather enjoyed putting her spelling skills to use.

The words to the old WW1 song, which Clara sang often, "There is work to be done, to be done, There's a war to be won, to be won." were certainly true at the Bradford farm. Or, any farm for that matter. There was no leisure time for the adults and very little for the children.

"I have a doozie of a job to do today,Buster. Have the twins put on their boots, we gotta move the outhouse." This was the assignment for this Saturday afternoon. Moving the outhouse was usually done yearly in the fall after the field work was done and when the wasps who nested in the corner were dormant.

A deep hole was dug alongside the small building and then the building was moved over the fresh hole. The dirt from the new hole was then used to cover the spot where the outhouse had previously rested. It took the three of them most of the afternoon to complete the job. Even with the digging being rather easy, hoisting the building up on steel rollers and then pushing it over took a lot of muscle.

After the outhouse was moved and leveled, new steps were added and the path extended, Clara then swept out the inside and placed the expired summer edition of the Sears and Roebuck catalog on the bench between the two holes. She also trimmed off the top of the heavy paper bag containing the lime which set on the floor in the corner. City folks merely pushed a handle after using the toilet and their deposit was flushed away to some unknown place. But country folks sprinkle their toilet with lime to keep the odor down and flies away, and it is "flushed" away once a year when the toilet is moved. She swept down the spider webs and disposed of the funny cylinder-like bee nests made of mud. It wasn't uncommon for her to use any leftover wallpaper to decorate the inside of the toilet. The front cover of the Saturday Evening Post was often pinned to the wall. It was really quite a "homey" little building despite its sub-freezing temperatures in winter and boiling heat in summer.

It was an unusually nice November day. Despite warm temperatures, nature and the livestock were getting ready for winter. The trees had shed their leaves and their bare branches were ready for the long winter that was sure to come. The cattle and horses had grown a heavy coat of fur and the chickens stayed closer to the coop and depended entirely on the corn that was shelled just for them. The farm was beginning its preparation for hibernation over the long cold winter that was predicted by the heavy furry caterpillars. To insulate the house from the brutal north winds that would surely come, Walter stacked straw around the house foundation while Clara stuffed strips of newspaper around the ill-fitting windows.

The deadline for shipping out Christmas boxes for those in service was fast approaching. Clara counted ration stamps for sugar and would soon start her baking and preparing special boxes to send to Junior and to Alden.

Chapter 29

Christmas Prayer Answered

The two-star flag was adjusted almost daily to make sure it hung straight. It beamed from the front window of the Bradford home, notifying the passersby that two of their boys were serving in the military. The twins were talking about joining the navy when they turned seventeen in December even though they would have to quit high school. Clara objected and it would take her signature before they could join at such a young age.

For now, it was time to get Christmas boxes ready to mail to Junior and Alden. Junior's must be mailed soon to assure it would reach him somewhere in Germany by Christmas. Alden's could wait since he was stationed in Florida for the time being. Sending them a couple weeks apart meant she would have the use of the upcoming sugar coupons for the second box. There never seemed to be enough sugar.

Clara busied herself about the kitchen, stirring up big yellow sugar cookies with a raisin in the center, and deep brown molasses cookies with a dab of jelly in the middle. The rich chocolate fudge bubbled in its pan while Clara put another stick of wood in the fire pit of the "Warm Morning" cooking range.

Junior's last V-mail letter said only that he was in Germany and was well. It also said that he had been promoted to Corporal. Clara didn't like the V-mail letters. They were only small copies of the real letters he wrote that were forwarded on to the Eaton Rapids address. They were on paper he never touched nor did he seal the envelope that held the contents. On the bright side, it was his handwriting and his personal messages to the family. There was little he could say without it being censored, but the family knew that for the time being he was well.

Clara wondered where in Germany he was, how close to the enemy lines he might be, and if he had a warm bed to sleep in at night. She wondered if he was safe from the enemy. Her common sense told her that a truck driver in Germany couldn't be too far from the fighting, and any place in Germany was not safe. She tried not to think abut the danger he might face. Instead, she worked on his Christmas box. Along with the cookies and fudge, she would include the most recent edition of Zane Grey's western novel, as well as a pair of warm wool socks she purchased from Davidson Woolen Mills. In one corner of the box, walnut meats were wrapped in wax paper and tied with string. In the other corner kernels of popcorn were wrapped in brown paper. Clara wasn't sure he would have a place to pop the corn, but she wanted him to have a sample of the fine crop the family grew in the garden. From Hafner's five and ten cent store she purchased a pound of hard candy in red, green and white strips. This was a tradition more than a favorite. It added a festiveness to the small box addressed to Cpl. Walter Bradford, Jr. in care of the Postmaster in New York, New York.

The usual weekly letter did not come from Junior. This happened from time to time and then two would arrive the following week.

Two weeks later she packed an identical box for Alden stationed in Florida. In place of the book, however, she enclosed recent issues of "Popular Mechanics" and in place of wool socks, she included several new white hankies. She had used all the available sugar coupons for the two Christmas boxes. She hoped she could save out enough sugar in the next two weeks for cookies and fudge for the remaining children still at home. They would, however, understand if there was no fudge with black walnut meats this year. Fighting the war and keeping our boys morale up was the most important issue on everyone's mind. The home front learned early on to do without. "Remember Pearl Harbor" was written on signs, in newspapers and magazines. There were constant reminders that our nation was at war.

No letters arrived from Junior. Clara reasoned that perhaps he was moving and could not write. This happened once before. It had been three weeks without a letter. The evening news talked about the fighting in Germany, and that the allies were driving back the enemy and making progress. Again, they told about the retreating Germans stringing wire across the roads, neck high. Several advancing U.S. truck drivers, not seeing the wire, had been decapitated. Clara prayed that one of those soldiers was not Junior. And yet, she knew they were someone's beloved sons.

Christmas came and there was still no letter from Junior. Clara started meeting the mailman at the road to make sure he had not overlooked the letters, or to look for any reason why the letters were not arriving. The mailman showed great concern too, and assured her that no letters arrived at the Post Office. "It could be the Christmas rush!" he tried to console her. The neighbors stopped by the house to inquire if a letter had arrived.

Clara barely spoke to anyone as she went about her work buried in grief. Even the twins could not bring her out of her depression with their usual jokes and antics. She was totally obsessed with the safety of her firstborn. Alden wrote that he was assigned to a ship and would be leaving port soon; he knew not where. He would take up his duties in the boiler room of the troop transport ship Anderson. Clara prayed for his safety. "What lies ahead for my boys?" she asked, but received no answer.

The highlight of the 1944 Christmas was Winona coming home. Chicken was served for dinner and Clara's spirits were somewhat lighter. She found comfort in the old saying "No news is good news." She would have certainly received a telegram by now if her worst fears had been realized.

Determined to keep tradition alive, Winona scrounged together enough sugar to make a batch of fudge and the twins cracked hickory nuts for the meats to be stirred into the brown, sweet candy. The Christmas tree, that stood in the corner of the living room, held very few presents. Only one or two small items for Bill and John who were too young to understand the impact of the war.

Christmas day passed. Winona went back to her apartment. The children had the entire week off between Christmas and

New Years before they returned to school. Two days after Christmas the twins would celebrate their seventeenth birthday. Joining the navy was uppermost in their minds, but since it needed their mother's signature, they hesitated to mention it at this time. Clara was in no mood to sign away two more of her boys to war.

The honking of the mailman's horn broke the silence of the gloomy household. Two short beeps and one extremely long. Clara's first thought was he was bearing bad news. But the horn continued to honk. She moved aside the two star flag and could see he was half out of the car door window waving several pieces of mail in his hand and with a smile that could not be concealed.

Clara rushed out the door, leaving it ajar. She waded through the snow without boots, hat or coat to accept the eagerly awaited mail. She held in her hands five letters from Junior - - - all with different dates. She barely heard the mailman call after her "The Christmas rush must of held 'em up." She didn't need a reason. She held the answer to her prayers in her hand.

Chapter 30

Barney and the Sled

The sun was shining and it was a bit warmer. The old folks called it "the January thaw." The huge icicles that hung on the corner of the house roof were yielding to the bright sun and warmer temperatures by sending tiny rivers of water down their long icy spines. The old timers also knew that the "thaw" would last only a day or two and then there would be plenty of winter weather left before spring.

The bright sun inspired Clara to plant tomato seeds, or at least look over the Burpee seed catalog that just arrived. She felt like digging in the earth. Common sense told her that she needed to wait a few more months for that. She was, however, making plans for the new batch of baby chicks that she raised each spring. The paper urged farmers to raise more poultry. "Poultry Fights For Freedom," the ads declared.

The twins were into a building project of their own. Not the usual airplane building project, this was a much bigger enterprise. In fact, they were in the barn constructing it, since it was too large for the house.

From a pile of used lumber stacked in the corner, they pulled out several boards. Their mission was to build a sled. One big enough for both Bill and John to ride on, and the horse could pull. From the bottom of the pile, they took a couple of two-by-fours that would work for the runners.

They pulled out the nails from the timber. Kyle straightened each one by placing it on the cement floor of the barn and pounding it straight with the hammer. Lyle searched the woodshed for the hand saw.

They worked away the afternoon; while one held, the other nailed, and while one grasped the other end, one sawed. They remembered when they were young kids how Dad would take them and Alden to the city dump, to dig through what others had thrown away. They would come home with wheels and axles, and pieces of metal perfect for some sort of a building project they might conjure up. Clara used to complain that their back yard was beginning to look like the dump. A visit to the dump today would find no metal pieces. Every little piece of old metal was now collected and used for the war effort.

They longed for Alden's advice when the finished sled seemed to be out of square. Alden usually helped with that type of problem or any other structural problem they might encounter with their building projects.

But Bill didn't notice if it was somewhat out of square, nor did he care. He saw that there was enough space to include little brother, John, and maybe even room for at least one of the neighbor kids.

For a trial run, the twins tried to push Bill up and down the driveway. They quickly realized that it was way too heavy for them, and besides the 2 x 4 runners were not sliding on the snow very well. In fact, not at all. It definitely needed to be pulled by a horse.

The next day being Sunday, Dad harnessed up old Barney. Barney hadn't been worked since last fall. He was old but he still had a lot of spirit. Dad was in hopes the horses would last at least for the duration of the war. After that, he would convert to tractor power.

Barney was eager to get back in his collar and get hooked up to something. The "spring thaw" was over and it was bitter cold and cloudy- - - a typical Michigan winter day.

Bill sat in the front of the sled and took the reins.

"Giddy ap, Barney."

He wiggled the reigns. Barney pulled as if the homemade sled, slightly out of square, was nothing. Bill took his solo run up the road past the first Swan's house, beyond the pig pen and past the second Swan house where he turned around and headed Barney toward home. This became the "parade route," as Bill called it.

At home he called for John. "Here, Johnny ride with me. Sit between my legs." On his second trip the pigs came to the fence to witness the big work horse pulling a five foot sled with the two children. They laughed and hollered with excitement.

It wasn't long before the two Swan children heard the commotion and, dressed in their snowsuits and boots, came to the road. "Can we ride, too?" they both asked as the horse and sled sped past.

The Swan children were Bill's best buddies. Howard was Bill's age while Audrey was two years older. Living across the road meant they were together almost every day. Of course, Bill would take them for a ride, but only one at a time.

"Whoa, Barney!" Bill pulled the reigns back.

"You ride first, Audrey. Sit behind."

Audrey did as instructed, but Howard thought he should be first.

"You can ride next," Bill called over his shoulder.

Bill looked for his mittens but could only find one. Apparently the mate had fallen out along the way. Clara usually had the younger children's mittens fastened together with a long string crocheted of wool yarn. Long enough to be attached to one mitten, extend up the coat sleeve across the back and down the other sleeve to attach to the remaining mitten. Keeping the mittens with the coat prevented them from being lost. These particular mittens were new for Christmas and Clara had not as yet had time to crochet the string.

The three of them rode the parade route, laughing and singing the familiar song "Jingle Bells." Even though there were no bells attached to Barney's harness, nor was he prancing as they visualized the horse in the song, nevertheless they were happy children content with their lot in life. Bill pulled his mittenless hand up the arm of his coat sleeve to keep it warm. Their faces tingled from the frigid wind.

Howard stood by the side of the road waiting his turn.

"You're next!" Bill called as they passed him to turn around in the Bradford yard.

They came back and stopped by the impatient Howard.

"Are you missing a mitten?" Howard taunted

"Na, na, na, na, na" he sang. "I threw it into the pig pen!"

New mittens didn't come as easy to the Bradford children as they did to the Swans. Bill did not see the humor in Howard's actions. In fact, Bill knew that he would probably not get another new pair, and to add to that Mom would be very upset.

"Money doesn't grow on trees!" he could hear her say between clenched teeth.

It only took a minute for Bill to respond. "I changed my mind- - you don't get to ride at all. Come on Audrey, get back on."

The rest of the afternoon was spent with the three riding the parade route, Bill in the middle holding the reigns and trying to overlook his one cold hand, with John in front and Audrey in the back. They rode up and down the road ignoring Howard who still stood at the side of the road, throwing snowballs at them when they passed.

The next day, after morning chores, Dad came into the house and announced "Barney is dead!"

When Bill got the news he was upset and wondered if he had done something that would cause his death. Billy thought over yesterday's event - -Barney never trotted, nor did he run. He merely walked his own pace. The load he pulled slid easily on the snow packed road. Why did he die? Could he have been responsible somehow?

"Well, he was just old." A man of few words, Dad, attempted to console his young son.

The sled, slightly out of square, never got used again. Walter sold a couple of cows and scraped together a down payment for a used, steel-wheeled, red Farmall F-20 tractor the next spring. The Bradford farm was converted to tractor power before the war was over.

Chapter 31

Tractor Farming and Baby Chicks

The twins had convinced Mom to sign their papers. They had a way of talking her into almost anything. They would finish their junior year at Olivet High School before going into the navy sometime during the summer. That meant they would quit school with only one more year to go. Clara sadly signed away her identical twins who brought so much joy and happiness to the Bradford household. The family would miss them terribly. As she placed her signature on each legal form she agonized over their departure, and wondered how Dad would manage without them. She couldn't let the farm and home responsibilities interfere with her sons' quest for new horizons. Joining the navy would be an adventure the seventeen-year-old boys, who had barely been out of the county, would love. "Join the Navy and See the World" is what the ads read. Clara would be replacing the two star flag in the window with one with four stars.

Perhaps Barney's death was a blessing in disguise. It forced Dad to convert to tractor power instead of using horses. To o his decision was that his main help, the remaining two o..st sons, would soon be leaving the farm. He had to get along without the boys, and a tractor would help.

Converting a farm to tractor power is not as simple as just buying a tractor. All the farm machinery was horse-drawn and would require modification for tractor use. Dad sawed the long tongues that once separated the two horses, from the corn planter, cultivator, hay mower and combine, and attached a heavy steel clevis to the shortened tongue of each implement in order to hook them to the draw-bar of the tractor. However, to plant corn, cultivate, mow hay and combine the grain it would now take two people. One to drive the tractor and one to ride the implement and operate the lift levers and row markers. But, there would be no wasted time in stopping to rest the tractor like the horses required from time to time.

Clara was making plans for the usual spring batch of chickens. She inspected the brooder coop and decided it would cost too much in kerosene fuel to try to keep it warm enough for baby chicks, since the building was in such a bad state of repairs. The paper was full of ads urging farmers to raise more poultry. Hansen Packing Company on West Knight Street advertised for more eggs and more poultry. "Help Feed Our Troops," the ads pleaded. The paper also urged folks to save paper bags, comic books for Percy Jones, and "Save tin cans and help bomb Tokyo," the ads read. Boy Scout Troop 52 was doing a waste paper pickup "to beat Japan." This was in addition to the bits of used metal and kitchen grease drained from cooking fatty pork sausage and bacon that each household was already saving.

She could help the war effort by raising extra chickens. She had a choice of waiting for the weather to warm up more so the chickens could survive in the brooder coop, or convert the boys' upstairs bedroom to a brooder coop and get the chicks early. If she waited for the weather, chances are by the time the chickens were ready for market so would many other farmer's chickens. With a glut on the market, the price would be down. But if she got them early, she would be ahead of the game.

So, the plan was set- - the upstairs bedroom would become a brooder coop for baby chicks. The Bradford family would help feed the troops and also make some needed extra money for themselves.

Early in March the twins moved their bed, and the empty one that Junior and Alden once used, to the parlor room downstairs, along with their workbench and dresser. Clara set about making the room ready for two hundred baby chicks that would come in the mail.

The stovepipe from the wood burner downstairs ran through the edge of the converted make-do brooder coop upstairs which radiated heat, but not enough for the tiny chicks. Expired license plates were nailed over the mouse holes in the floor, and after laying down several layers of newspapers, an umbrella-like kerosene heater was installed in the center of the room. The chicks could huddle underneath the warm outstretched arms of the heater much like under their own mothers' wings. Watering devices were screwed onto two-quart canning jars. When filled and inverted they served as drinking fountains for the baby birds. Various long metal containers were filled with mash. Each container had a cover with at least two dozen little holes across the top, just big enough for a baby chick to put in its head but too small to squeeze in its body.

She was all ready for them the day the mailman brought the boxes to the farm. Four boxes with air holes in the sides, full of chirping little black puffy balls known as baby chicks.

Clara opened each box and with John's help gently lifted the complaining little chicks out onto the fresh newspapered floor and into their big new world.

"Why are they crying so?" John asked

"Well, they miss their mamma," Clara responded, "and they are hungry, too."

Actually these chicks never saw their mother. They were born in a big incubator somewhere else, packaged and shipped not only to this farm but to many other farms around the country, to whoever placed an order.

It took some time before they calmed down and stopped making so much commotion. As soon as they discovered the food, water and the warmth from the heater, they settled into their upstairs home.

"Now, you kids needn't tell people we have chickens in the house," Clara instructed the children at the supper table that night. She had mixed emotions, she was both embarrassed and proud at the same time. She didn't like the idea of a flock of chickens being raised in the upstairs bedroom, but on the other hand she was delighted to be getting a head start on her batch of spring chickens.

Tending to the chickens was an easy chore for Clara. She merely carried a milk pail full of water up the stairs each morning and evening to replenish their drinking water. From the hundred pound sack of mash in the corner that the twins carried up, she scooped out more food for the feeders. Every few days she rolled up the top layer of poopy newspaper, exposing the fresh sheets beneath. The chicks were warm, eating, drinking and growing fast, just the way they were supposed to.

As they grew larger their noise grew louder, too. No one could sleep in the house after daylight. In just a few short weeks they had changed from cute little black puff balls to much larger birds with feathers, and the small space they once occupied now covered the entire room. They now hopped on top of the feeders, onto the window sills, and walked all over the bags of feed that lined one wall. And their poop, which also got larger, was everywhere. When the door was opened, they flapped their wings and made such a commotion that it stirred up all sorts of dust. The windows were so clouded with soil, it was difficult to see the morning sun. It was time to move the chickens outdoors.

By now the weather was warm enough and Clara got the big chicken coop ready for the birds. They were ready to be outside, to scratch in the earth and explore the farm.

That evening when the chickens were asleep, each family member gathered up a few and took them outside to their new home. It took many trips back and forth, upstairs and down, but the surviving 200 birds were finally in their coop where they would grow even larger.

As Clara closed the coop's door, after the last batch was safely placed inside, she felt good that they would help feed the troops, including the Bradford boys.

Chapter 32

FDR's Sudden Death
V-E Day

The tide of war was quickly turning in favor of an Allied victory in Europe. The Allied forces had pushed through France and into Germany. Berlin would soon be the second of the Axis capitals to fall. In the Pacific theater the American flag had been raised over the island of Iwo Jima, but the Japanese Premier Suzuki announced that Japan will fight to the very end rather than accept unconditional surrender.

Hopes were high that the war in Europe would soon be over. Clara felt better about her twin sons leaving for the navy. Perhaps their stay would be short. She read in the paper where Howard Umbarger had been released from a German prisoner-of-war camp somewhere in Germany. There was no word as to when he would return home.

That April 12th evening the radio was turned on for the evening news. The war news was so hopeful, especially with the possible defeat of the Germans. The war with Japan was going our way and we were winning battles close to the

Japanese homeland. But the stubborn Japanese were not going to surrender.

"Dad, Dad, listen, listen!" Clara had her ear to the radio. "The President has died! "

"And the war is almost over. What a shame," Dad responded.

The evening news reported that President Franklin Delano Roosevelt, better known as FDR, had died suddenly while in Warm Springs, Georgia.

The 31st President of the United States was 63 years of age at his death. As soon as word was received, Vice President Harry Truman was sworn into office.

The nation was in mourning. A funeral train brought Roosevelt's body from Warm Springs to Washington. Thousands of people gathered along the tracks just to view the train, draped in black, slowly making its way to the Capital. Although copper was rationed as part of the war effort, a copper-lined coffin was built for his internment. A horse drawn caisson brought the body from Union Station to the Capital in a long slow funeral procession. Thousands and thousands crowded the parade route in solemn tribute to a president who had brought the nation through two crises, the Great Depression, and World War two. After funeral ceremonies, his body was again placed on the special train for a last ride to his home in Hyde Park, New York.

On the same day of FDR's death, the Allies liberated Buchenwald and Belsen concentration camps. Auschwitz had already been liberated by the Soviet troops. Terrible news was starting to filter out from these camps of the horrific treatment of the Jews.

Events were happening fast and the radio was left on all day at the Bradford house for any breaking news. Mussolini, Dictator of Italy, was captured and hanged by his own people; Adolf Hitler committed suicide in a hidden bunker under Berlin, and the German forces surrendered unconditionally to the Allies. May 8, 1945, Victory in Europe! The Allies victory was celebrated in Washington D.C. and in Capitals around the world.

It was also a time for joy and celebration in Eaton Rapids! The town folks gathered on Main Street. The honking car horns and Horner's whistle, which normally blew at noon time and quitting time, blasted long and extra loud the good news. The Bradford family reserved their celebration for total victory-- when Japan would surrender unconditionally, too. Now, on to Japan for a final victory.

Outside Bill and John were playing war with the neighbor children. Clara could hear their happy voices as they hid behind bushes and trees and pointed their wooden guns, the twins had made, at imaginary enemies. The Bradford children never pointed their make-believe guns at any person. Dad had told them only once, but the message stayed forever. "Never point a gun at anyone unless you intend to shoot them." Even when they argued that it was only a play gun, Dad's firm reply was the same. "It doesn't matter, never aim a gun at anyone."

And so, they fought the war. "Watch out! That yellow Jap has you in his sights.!"

The children had already switched from "Get that dirty Kraut." to "Get that yellow Jap!" The final push was on.

A letter from Junior announced that he was leaving Germany and was being shipped somewhere else. He did not say where; he couldn't have said even if he knew. Common sense would tell you that he was headed for the big push on Japan. Alden's ship was making its way to the Pacific, too.

"Please Lord, keep them safe and bring them home soon." This was Clara's silent prayer.

One of the first items the Twin's sent home from Pearl Harbor was a grass skirt for sister Jean.

Chapter 33

Twins Leave for the Navy
The Milking Lesson

The twins seemed more solemn tonight as they dumped their pails of milk into the strainer perched on top of the milk can. They finished the milking early and now all that was left was to let the cows out and clean the stanchions. They were both happy and sad at the same time. Happy to be leaving the farm tomorrow to wherever the navy would send them, and sad because they were leaving the safety and serenity of the farm and their family. Funny how they were both happy and sad about the same thing- - leaving home in the morning.

Uncle Harry, Aunt Eva and Dean were over for dinner for the usual send-off. Winona was home, too. The boys were embarrassed at the extra fuss made over them, but aunts, uncles and cousins were always welcome guests in the Bradford home.

The next morning there were no wristwatches for departing gifts, only hugs and handshakes as Kyle and Lyle, along with other young men, boarded the Greyhound Bus headed for Detroit.

Clara held each of them just a little longer. She could not speak for fear of crying. They understood and gently hugged her back. She noticed how strong and handsome they were with their dark wavy hair combed back to reveal young innocent faces that had been tempered only with the peacefulness and love of their family and not at all hardened for war.

"Dad, I willed my milk pail to Billy," Lyle said in a humble attempt at humor.

"He's only seven, but I bet he can learn to milk," Dad responded with a chuckle. "Now you boys take care of yourselves."

"We'll write as soon as we can," they both said in unison. They waved and smiled their identical broad smiles which exposed their perfect teeth, and then the door to the bus closed behind them and they were gone.

Grandma had supper ready when the rest of the family got home. The table was set for only six. Clara looked at the shrinking table and ran to her bedroom where she wept behind closed doors. "How can we endure this hardship? How can this family manage without the boys?"

Her answer came when little Bill, now the oldest boy at home, slid the bedroom door open, saying in grownup fashion, "Come on Mom, everything is going to be OK."

Soon after their departure, letters starting arriving. Nothing inspired nor boosted Clara's morale more than to have a letter from one of her boys. One of the first was from Kyle. "Lyle learned his lesson this morning. Remember when Alden told us never to volunteer for anything? Well, I guess Lyle didn't hear that. Anyway this morning they asked if any one would like to learn to fly. Lyle's hand flew up before I could get to him. So do you know what he spent the day doing? Dive bombing is what they call it, when you have a pole with a nail in the end and run around the area "diving" at pieces of paper and other stuff which are then put in a bag that hangs from his shoulder with a strap. Lyle spent the day cleaning up the grounds instead of relaxing and writing letters like the rest of us. I bet he won't volunteer again!"

Clara chuckled at their innocence.

He closed with, "And, oh Mom, it looks like Lyle and I will be able to attend classes and get our high school diplomas."

She unrolled a new four-star flag and replaced the two-star flag that hung in the window. "I have no more children to give," she murmured as she tacked it in place. On the bright side, the war news was so very encouraging. After victory in Europe all the war effort was now focused on Japan. Everyone hoped they would surrender soon, but every indication was that they would fight until the very last.

Seven-year-old Bill, keeping his promise that "everything would be all right," removed Lyle's milk pail from the stack on the reservoir of the kitchen range and followed Dad to the barn.

"We're going to have to get you some barn boots," Dad said, knowing that rubber was not available and that a pair of the twins' boots would somehow have to be made to fit his small feet. The solution was that Bill wore his shoes inside the boots, which were intended to be worn with only heavy socks.

Bill soon discovered that milking cows was not nearly as easy as he had thought. He had watched the others sit beside the cow and pull its teats while a steady stream of milk flowed into the pail, making a rhythmic sound. It seemed simple.

He pulled up the milk stool and placed the pail between his little knees and began to pull. Small squirts finally came. But he was determined and kept squeezing and pulling, just like Dad told him. When the cow decided he had had plenty of time to get the milk, she started to fidget, first switching her tail into Bill's intent face and finally by stepping into the pail with her right hind foot.

Dad came to his rescue, but Bill wouldn't give up. He was determined to learn how to milk the cows just like his older brothers did.

It took a while, but he finally got the procedure down pretty good for such a young child and could milk one cow while Dad milked the remaining seven.

He could hardly wait to take his pail of milk to the house to show Mom what he did all by himself. He picked up the pail with his right hand and proceeded to the house. With each little step the milk slopped over the edge, onto his leg and down inside his boot. The spilled liquid, warm and sticky, attracted the flies immediately. Half-way to the house, he sat the pail on the ground to consider just how to carry a pail of milk properly. The boys never slopped milk! "Perhaps," he thought, " if I carry it with both hands and straddle the pail, that would work." After several attempts with the new procedure, which slopped milk on both legs and down the tops of both boots, it was deemed hopeless, too.

"Billy, Billy!" Dad called from the barn. "Judas Priest, let me show you how to carry milk. You ain't gonna have any left at this rate! The secret is balance. You hafta carry a pail in each hand. Here, try this!" Dad handed him his half-filled pail and urged Bill to pick one up in each hand.

Bill did as instructed and completed the task, surprised that no more milk was slopped. From then on he took two milk pails to the barn with him and filled each half-full.

The atmosphere seemed lighter that evening. The war news was in the Allies' favor. Clara was lighthearted as they gathered around the radio to listen to Amos and Andy and laugh at the Kingfish's latest scheme to get rich. It was followed by Fibber McGee and Molly and thirty minutes of whimsical fun at Wistful Vista, an imaginary town located somewhere nearby.

It was good to hear Clara laugh.

Chapter 34

The Shopping Spree

"Why don't ya ride with me into town, Buster?" Dad seemed to realize that Clara needed to get her mind off her boys, and get away from the farm if only for a couple of hours.

"While I'm at the mill you could do a little window shopping in town," he continued. "Why don't ya buy yourself a new hat?"

"How frivolous is that?" Clara tartly responded. There was hardly enough money to buy sugar and flour, why would she spend a dollar on a silly hat, that should be spent on a dozen other necessary things?

"Come on, Buster, it'll do ya good," he urged.

She couldn't help but agree that going into town would be fun. Trying on hats they couldn't afford would lighten her heart. Grandma would be there when the younger children got home from school, so she decided to go.

She re-pinned strands of hair that had fallen from the bun at the back of her neck, then removed her apron and put on the best dress she owned. Finally she checked her purse to make sure she had the family's ration books. Once outside she hopped into the passenger side of the dusty old truck. Dad noticed she had a youthful bounce to her step. He smiled. The back of the truck was filled with grain to be ground at the mill for the milking cows.

The truck trip to Eaton Rapids, over the dusty, bumpy dirt roads, was traveled as usual without conversation. The rattling of the ill-fitting doors, and sundry other loose parts, made it impossible to hear a normal conversation. That left time for Clara to consider her lot in life. Surely the Lord had provided her with healthy, lively children for which she was so very thankful. Her thoughts wandered immediately to Junior on his way to the Pacific and Alden, too, who was on a ship headed in the same direction. Even the twins were on their way to Pearl Harbor where they would work as C-Bs(Navy Construction Battalion) cleaning up the mess the Japanese invasion left. She prayed the Japanese would surrender soon, but they had vowed to fight to the last man. She included in her prayers the safety of her boys, as well as the safety of all the young men who were represented by the stars in the windows of the houses they passed.

Even though her boys were out of her care, she found comfort in their letters, which were always cheerful. She could, however, detect that they were homesick. Or, did she hope they were? They were healthy, but missed her good cooking, and always asked how the younger ones were getting along and how the farm was doing.

When they got into town with its paved streets, conversation could take place.

"I'll meet ya here in front of the A&P 'bout three." Dad stopped the truck with an annoying weak squeal of the brakes. Clara walked south to Marie's Style Shop.

For two hours Clara was a carefree woman, trying on hats and imagining herself a happy-go-lucky lady of stature. She convinced herself that if she found a perfect hat she would consider buying it. That would give her purpose in shopping, and she would feel less guilty for the time she wasted.

She had read Marie's weekly ads in the *Eaton Rapids Journal.* "Dress Well - - Lift the Morale" and "A Woman Without a Hat is like a Picture Without a Frame."

She gently pushed open the glass door and stepped inside. Immediately she realized she was out of her league in this upscale dress shop. She felt like a frumpy farmwife in her simple cotton-print dress. One glance in the full length mirror and she saw where her once slim, shapely figure had been replaced with a full "matronly" look which was the result of hard work and giving birth to nine children. Her varicose veins protruded from under her only pair of nylon hose.

She moved quickly to a shoulder-high mirror where the hats were located. The reflected image was a pretty face with shiny ivory, flawless skin. Clara never used makeup and the stress lines about her mouth and eyes were becoming visible. "I earned these wrinkles," she often remarked. Her blue eyes twinkled with excitement as she placed one hat after the other over her graying hair.

The large brimmed fancy hats were no longer in vogue. Due to the war most hats were simpler with much smaller brims. She carefully placed the navy blue straw on the top of her head and spread the thin veil over her forehead, just below her eyes. She turned to the side and admired the big artificial flower that was gracefully perched to the side. The flower matched the color of her eyes and made them appear even a deeper blue. The sales clerk cocked the hat slightly to the left and a bit forward, and pointed out that so doing was "very fashionable."

"Oh, this hat is you!" the clerk gushed. "It is designed by a famous Paris milliner, you know."

It was a beautiful hat and Clara was indeed a pretty woman.

The ad was right, the pretty new hat did indeed "lift her morale." As she turned from left to right viewing her image in all directions, she imagined for a moment that she was the wife of a well-to-do businessman, and money was plentiful. Feeling silly over such thoughts, she imagined that the farm would produce an outstanding crop and extra money would be available to purchase such a frivolous thing. She tried another hat that cupped her face in such a fashion that it accentuated her attractive features. But the one with the blue flower was her favorite. The price tag read $3.99.

Realizing that her husband was anything but a well-to-do man and $3.99 was too much to spend, even if the crops produced a heavy yield, she thanked the clerk and went on up the street . Going north to the Vaughn store and then on to Webb's, she walked past the West Cafe. The aroma of food reminded her of home, supper and all her children gathered around the big oval table in the kitchen. She smiled and quickened her step.

She stopped to look in Alt's store window where on display were pictures of many of the service men from the area. Mr. Alt advertised he would display pictures of service men and women, if they were brought in. Clara made a mental note to drop her boys' pictures off.

She felt more at home in the Vaughn store and Webb's Department Store. These stores were where she bought work clothes for Dad and overalls for the boys. From these stores she had chosen yard goods for making aprons and other clothing articles for the girls in the family- - that was before printed feed bags. Today she was looking at their hats. She tried on one after another. They, too, were adorned with artificial flowers. Even with a price tag of $1.99, none measured up to the one in Marie's.

She realized she might just make do with her old hat, if she simply purchased a new flower for decoration. Clara was good at making do. With the decision made, she crossed Main Street, to Hafners 5 & 10 cent store to see what they had in artificial flowers. The clock in the window of Boyce's Bazaar reminded her she had very little time left.

At the back of the dime store among the assortment of lovely single flowers, she found a blue one to match her eyes. She visualized it perched on the side of her black straw and was pleased with the image she conjured up.

After making the 10 cent purchase, she looked across Main Street where Dad was already parked in front of the A & P just like he said he would be. Dad was a man of his word even in the smallest matters.

"Did you see 'em, Buster?" Dad asked when she opened the truck door.

"See who?"

"There must have been a hundred of them. They stopped the traffic and everything!"

"Dad, who stopped the traffic?" she insisted.

"It must have been the graduating class. They were wearing black robes. They snake danced all the way down Main Street. They caused quite a commotion." He chuckled.

Clara placed her purchase on the seat. "I gotta run into the A&P to pick up a couple cakes of yeast. I'll only be a minute."

"Hurry Buster, remember it takes longer to do the chores these days."

Once in the truck and on the way home, Clara reminisced over her "shopping spree." Dad was right, it did her good to get away for an afternoon to paved streets and sidewalks with store front windows on either side of the street, displaying new items to tempt the shopper- - away from the war and away from the farm. She hummed her favorite tune and waved to folks along the way.

As they neared the farm she started thinking of other things- - like getting supper for the family. Grandma would have the potatoes peeled, as she always did. And perhaps the mail brought another letter from one of her boys. She found herself eager to get home.

She opened her small sack. " Oh, Dad, see my new hat." she shouted above the noise of the truck.

Walter looked at the blue artificial flower, smiled and reached over and gently patted her knee.

West side of Main Street looking North

West Side of Main Street looking South

East Side of Main Street looking North

Chapter 35

Japan Surrenders

It was a typical hot August day when the radio announced the news, through static and network confusion. The war was over! The first report could not be confirmed and had to be retracted, but it was finally confirmed - - Japan had unconditionally surrendered!!! It was three months after victory was declared in Europe. The war was over!

It took two atomic bombs to finally convince Japan to surrender. A lone B-29 named the "Enola Gay" left Tinian across the bay from Saipan early that August morning in utter secrecy. President Truman, after much soul searching, reluctantly made the final decision to use ultimate power to force the Japanese war lords to their knees. No one knew for sure what would happen or how much destruction would result from an atomic air explosion, since the bomb was only tested once at ground level in New Mexico.

The first bomb was dropped on Hiroshima on August 6, 1945 after the Japanese refused to accept the Potsdam Declaration which demanded an unconditional surrender by Japan. This was a high security level secret bomb called the "little Boy." It had the explosive equivalent of 20,000 tons of high explosives. It created massive destruction for several miles from ground zero.

The Japanese War Council was still debating what to do, three days after the first bomb was dropped. The United States, hearing nothing from Japan, dropped a second atom bomb on August 9th over the city of Nagasaki. Still the world heard nothing, though the Japanese had begun secret talks with Russia and the United States. After suffering so serious a blow, it was difficult to understand why they did not immediately surrender. Apparently, there was much consternation among Japanese leaders as to what to do. Some wanted immediate surrender, others wanted to continue fighting, still others feared for the safety of their emperor. Finally, realizing they had no other choice, the Japanese surrendered unconditionally.

Clara recalled reading in the Eaton Rapids Journal just last week an ad that asked "Would you like to help bomb Tokyo? Save tin cans". She mused to herself that saving tin cans, pieces of string, paper bags, hunks of metal, cooking fat, newspapers and milk-weed pods, would no longer be necessary. Another ad read "Boy Scouts Troop 52 waste paper pickup now to beat Japan." Still another ad in the same paper asked its readers to "save comic books for Percy Jones." Saving items for the wounded veterans at the Battle Creek veterans hospital, and others across the nation, would not cease with the end of the war but would go on for many years to come.

The Main Street of Eaton Rapids was packed with vehicles with horns blaring and people hanging out the windows, riding on the fenders and the running boards shouting the good news. They heaped fuel to the huge bonfire at the corner of Main and Hamlin Streets while the celebrators banged together anything they could find to make a noise- - - the louder the better. Complete strangers were hugging each other. Some laughed while others had tears streaming down their cheeks. Those who lived in the country packed the kids in the back of their trucks, left the cows unmilked and drove to town for the celebration! The news had spread like wildfire and the party phone lines were jammed. Eaton Rapids was a madhouse of jubilant people. This was the scene all over the nation. Large, small and in-between cities all celebrated in the same manner, with sirens blaring, bonfires blazing, church bells ringing and firecrackers exploding wherever they could be found.

The end of the war meant Junior who had been reassigned from the European theater of war, would not be disembarking onto the Japanese shores, but would be returning home instead.

Clara thought perhaps the cancellation of this invasion saved his life and thousands of other U.S. soldiers who were waiting off the shore of the Japanese homeland for the invasion.

"Oh Dad! Our boys will be coming home!" Clara could hardly contain her excitement.

"I know, Buster," was his simple reply fighting back tears of joy.

Junior and Alden would be home, but the twins needed to complete their enlistment period. Clara hoped it would be cut short now that the war was over.

Even though she was thankful for her boys' safety, she grieved for all those innocent people who lost their lives from the bombs' explosions. But then, one could never forget Pearl Harbor when thousands lost their lives from Japan's sneak attack. Or the tens of thousands who died on jungle islands and open seas while fighting the Japanese onslaught. Not to mention those U. S. and British soldiers who died in Japanese prison camps and on the Bataan death march. Everyone loses during war. It was said that had the atomic bomb not been used, the Pacific war would have dragged on for months, and perhaps years, resulting in the deaths of hundreds of thousands of Americans and even more Japanese who would have fought the invaders with a ferocity much greater than seen on Okinawa and Iwo Jima where tens of thousands died. President Truman, it is estimated, saved one to two million lives by ending the war quickly.

Clara checked on her three sleeping children before going to bed herself. Safe in their beds they were oblivious to the historical events that were taking place, and how the world would be altered forever. No one could possibly dream of the changes the invention and use of one bomb, the "little boy," could possible make. She prayed that this new power would help to prevent future wars.

Chapter 36

Graduation

The letter was addressed to Mrs. Walter Bradford and was from Miss A. Fern Persons, Principal of the Walton Township Unit School.

Clara's mind raced as she fumbled to rip open the white envelope. "Could that Jean have skipped school again?" She wondered out loud. She hardly thought so since it was such a traumatic experience for Jean, the one and only time she and her girlfriends left school to attend a baseball game in Bellevue.

"Your four brothers are fighting for our country and here you are skipping school," Is what the stern and rigid principal, A. Fern Persons said to a weeping, bewildered ninth grader. "What do you think they would think of their little sister?"

"I'm sorry. I'm sorry. I'll never do it again!" was all that Jean could blubber.

Clara looked for a knife to aid in opening the curious envelope. "It certainly can't be Jean." she finally concluded as she unfolded the single sheet of paper.

It read:

Mrs. Bradford:

Your twin sons, Lyle and Kyle, have successfully completed their high school studies and are eligible to receive their diplomas at the regular graduation exercise on June 2, 1946, at 7pm.

I realize they are serving our country and will not be able to attend. Would you please accept their diplomas in their stead?

A chair will be reserved for you and your husband on the main floor of the gymnasium where the exercise will be held. I will call you up front to receive their diplomas that will be given out in alphabetical order.

Your boys are to be congratulated for completing their studies while at the same time serving our country.

Sincerely,

A. Fern Person, Principal

With the letter clasped in her hand, Clara ran to the field where Dad was fitting the land in preparation for corn planting. She couldn't wait for him to come in for supper.

"Look Dad! Look Dad!" She waved the letter and shouted above the roar of the tractor. "Lo and behold, the twins will be graduating after all!" She was so determined that her children graduate from high school. Neither she nor Dad had the opportunity to complete more than the 8th grade.

Dad shut off the engine and climbed down from the big red International Farmall and took the letter from her hand. It seemed so quiet when the tractor was idle, as if the very beating of your heart could be heard. A flock of robins snatched up insects and angleworms from the fresh earth.

After reading the letter, he grasped Clara at the waist and swung her around holding her tight. That show of affection was never displayed in the house in front of the children. They both laughed. It was obvious that Dad was happy too.

The whole family got spiffed up in their best clothes for the event. Clara situated her little black straw with the new blue flower just so on her head. Dad drove the family to Olivet for the graduation exercise.

The other children sat in the balcony where they had a clear view of the event. The high school band was assembled on the main floor near the stage. Several rows of chairs were ribboned off, reserved for the junior class. The maroon stage curtains were wide open revealing empty chairs, one for each graduate and for the speakers.

Band Director, Sam Robinson raised his baton and the band commenced to play Pomp & Circumstance. The crowd hushed and the robed seniors marched down the center of the gymnasium and up the temporary steps onto the stage. As they took their seats, the speakers emerged from the side stage and sat in their respective chairs.

To Clara it was all a blur until the end of the program when diplomas were passed out. Miss Persons stood behind the stack of rolled-up documents and commenced to call off names. Since it was done alphabetically, the Bradford boys were one of the first.

"Accepting the diplomas for her sons, Lyle and Kyle Bradford, who are serving our country in the navy, is Mrs. Walter Bradford."

Clara thought her knees would surely give way as she walked down the center aisle, up the steps and onto the stage. As she accepted the two diplomas the crowd broke out in applause.

Her letter that evening to her two boys was full of every detail, or as much as she could recall, of graduation. She was indeed a proud mother and prayed for their safe return.

Chapter 37

War Heroes Return

Her boys came home in the order that they had left. Only they went as boys and came home men with experiences they kept hidden in their hearts and never spoke about. With a new awareness they matured into men much older than their ages indicated or could conceive.

Winona's husband was home too. He came home to his wife and their apartment in Battle Creek and immediately went back to the job he left at Grand Trunk Western Railroad, working in the huge locomotive repair and maintenance shops.

Each came home with the sense of fulfilling his patriotic responsibility. They asked for no rewards or recognition, they only wanted to get back to work and get on with the life they left behind years before. Trapped deep inside Junior's blue eyes were war atrocities his young eyes should never have witnessed. The vivid pictures would play and replay in his mind. As years went by the images became blurred and somewhat faint, but they occupied a prominent place in his subconscious for the rest of his life.

The atmosphere of the entire country was suddenly more uplifting and lighthearted. *The Eaton Rapids Journal* announced on the front page that Scott Munn and his band were returning to regular concerts on the Island Park. And the Victory Hall announced dances every Saturday night. This was a sure indicator that the community would soon be back to normal. There was a demand for all sorts of items unrelated to guns, jeeps, tanks, bombers and the hundreds of other war-related items. There was a great demand in every city, small town and rural community now for new household furniture and appliances, sparkling new automobiles, for car parts and tires, farm machinery and housing.

Buildings were freshly painted, long put-off repairs made, and indoor and outdoor spaces created for a new outlook on life. And a major building boom erupted in places like Levittown, New York, where planned community and "cookie cutter" reproductions escalated to fill the pent-up demand for new housing. Tens of thousands of new houses sprang up for returning service men and women and their families.

The country was getting back to normal production. The Gamble Store advertised a new Coronado wringer washing machine for sale and Bromeling and Foster advertised brand new 1946 Fords now on display, with improved horsepower from 90 to 100. Steward Chevrolet boasted the new 1946 Chevrolet was pre-engineered to lead all others in performance. McNamara Auto Sales advertisements pointed with pride to an automatic Hydra-matic drive with no clutch pedal on the latest Oldsmobile. The last automobile of any kind had been built in early 1941. Everyone, it seemed, wanted a new car and the waiting list for new automobiles greatly outnumbered production.

New package foods in colorful wrappings became available, along with fragrant soaps and nylon stockings. Rationing books were put in drawers or thrown away with the hope of never using them again. One could buy as many pairs of shoes as could be afforded, and the stickers on the automobile windshields, indicating how much gas could be purchased at one time, were scraped off with a razor blade.

It was close to Christmas when the last Bradford boy came home. Strong and mature, their boyish ways and days were over. Even the twins at nineteen were no longer boys building model airplanes, instead they were talking about learning to fly real airplanes on the GI bill.

Once again the table was set for ten. Except on Sunday it was set for twelve. Whether they came home or not, the table was always set for Bob and Winona. They hardly missed a Sunday. It grieved Clara so to remove the plates one by one as her children left. But now they were all home! The horrible war was over and all the plates, including the cracked and chipped ones, were back on the table.

Supper was enjoyed as usual. With meat rationing gone the Bradford family often had meat for supper twice a week instead of just on Sunday. Occasionally Clara would purchase a beef roast at the A & P or Hauschs. A large beef roast was intended to last for two meals. One as a delicious roast with mashed potatoes and gravy, and for the second meal the leftovers were made into beef stew, oftentimes with baking powder biscuits on top.

Conversation around the dinner table tonight was in whispers and in coded signals. It was just three days before Christmas and it was obvious the boys were doing a lot of planning for the big occasion. The bleak Christmases during the war years were only a memory. The returning men would spend the day surrounded by loved ones in a warm house with lots of food instead of the war-torn countryside of Germany, or the bowels of a troop ship, zig-zagging across the ocean to avoid mines and enemy torpedoes. It would be the first Christmas the children would all be home in over four years.

After supper dishes were done Clara settled back in her large overstuffed chair. Any other night she would be doing some mending, reading the paper or writing letters. But this evening was different. She just sat and inhaled the beauty around her- - her children, their laughter and excited talk. The aroma of the cedar Christmas tree in the corner permeated the room. The fire in the heating stove sent its reflections dancing through its celluloid window about the warm, cozy room.

They were all there. Dad and Grandma and all the children were with her in the living room warming themselves by the wood heating stove. Through the din of their laughter and conversation she felt peace. Peace and joy that could not be explained even if she could find the words. She was warmed as though she had been wrapped in her mother's shawl. The crackling of the fire was scarcely heard by the others, but to her it was like music. She closed her eyes to drink in her pleasurable surroundings. She wished this very moment could last forever. She silently thanked the Lord for her answered prayers. Not only were her four sons and her son-in-law home and safe, but her three brothers were back from the horrible war unscathed and in the family home up north. Glancing at the four-star flag in the window she thanked God once more that the stars were all blue. Many mothers were not as lucky.

Dad reached in his pocket for his harmonica. Running the full length of the scales, back and forth before breaking out in rousing renditions of the only song he knew, "Turkey in the Straw." The others sang, or tried to sing- - the Bradfords were not known for their musical talent or abilities. However, young John showed a real aptitude for music.

The children were full of "remember when" stories accompanied by laughter and good-hearted bantering. The Bradford family had waited a long time for this very moment, when they would all be together once again.

Unnoticed by the others, Clara got up from her chair and went to the window. She pulled back the sheer curtain exposing the red, white and blue flag. Pulling the tack that held it firmly in place, she rolled up the four-star flag and without hesitation tossed it into the crackling fire. A sudden puff of white smoke and bright flame signaled an end to a war weary world.

The End

Local Eaton Rapids Men & Women who served in the Armed Forces during WWII

* Indicates those who gave supreme sacrifice.

Army

Melvin Aldrich

W. H. Alexander

Warren Anderson

Zelest Andrea

Bernard Andreas

John Andreas

Donald S. Ashley

Harold Ashley

Walter Ashley

Eugene Baker

Raymond Baker

Max O. Bartlett

Claude Basing

Clarence Battley

Robert Beasore

Charles Ray Beck

Donald Beck

John Becker

Harry J. Bellows

Charles Bennett

James M. Bennett

H. R. Bentley

Clifford Biggs

John Bird

* Judson Bishop

Lawrence F. Blackett

Maynard Blankenburg

* Veryl L. Bollman

Max Bollman

* Charles Bostedor

Allen Bowen

Claud Bowen

Wayne L. Bowen

Wayne D. Bradford

Walter M. Bradford, Jr.

Chester Bradley

Roy M. Bramble

Charles Bright
Alton Brown
Howard Brown
Thompson Browne
Enoch D. Buck
John Buck
Arsene Buckliear
Merle Burker
Cary E. Burns
Willard Burt
Walter L. Bush
Alfred J. Byron
Raymond Byron
Chales Cambric
Albert P. Campbell
Dale Campbell
Earl Cantine
Harry Card
Harvey R. Carpenter
Leo J. Carr
Leo Carrier
Ivery Carter
Duard Casler

* Maurice Chadwick
Richard Charlefour
Reid Cheney
John Cherry
Neil Childs
Harold Claflin
Chauncey Clark
Joseph A. Clark
Richard J. Clark
Robert G. Clark
Freddie L. Clarke
Albert Clegg
Dewey Coffey
Jack J. Coffey
Bruce G. Cook
James Cook
David Corbin
Claudie Crandall
Mike Crawley
Noland Culver
Donald J. Cupp
Ector Dandurand
Alexander Davidson

Gayle Davis
William Davis
Clark Davison
Robert Davison
Herbert Decker
Fred E. Derby
* Lawrence DeView
Floyd DeWaters
Marion DeWaters
Ivan Dodge
Robert Dodge
Roy Dodge
Albert Dowd
* Robert E. Doxtader
Morris Doxtader
* Arlo W. Dralle
Wayne Dralle
Archibald R. Earl
Florous E. Edick
Clayton D. Elston
Herbert K. Elston
Virgil Elston
Carl Emory

Victory Faber
Howard Fairbanks
Jack Fairbanks
Douglas Ferguson
Robert J. Ferguson
Howard Figley
Ralph Figley
Lewis Finch
Raymond F inch
Robert Forward
Floyd D. Fowler
Alfred French
Charles French
Ralph L. Fuller
Robert W. Fuller
Robert W. Galvin
Vernon Garrison
Kurt Gemalsky
John D. Gephart
Albert Getter
Robert Gillett
Sidney Goff
Alfred N. Grimes

Max Grimes

Virginia Grimes

Lyle Grindling

Edward A. Gruber

James Haley

Bruce Hall

Fred A. Halsey

Russell Halsey

Donald Harris

Gerald J. Harshey

Kenneth Harshey

Robert Harshey

Wells Hathaway

Wendell Hathaway

Carl Hayden

Robert R. Haynes

Sam M. Haynes

Leslie Hayter

Claude W. Henry

Robert Herrick

Harland Hicks

Ralph Higdon

* Robert S. Higgins

Kenneth Higgins

Wayne Hock

Cliff Hoffman

Kenneth Hoffman

R. C. Holcomb

George Holley

Ottmar Holley

Chester J. Holley

Guy M. Holwig

William S. Horner

George W. Hudson

Donald Hunt

Clare Huntington

Earl Husted

Max Hutchinson

Don G. Hutton

* Duane Jackson

Fred A. Jackson

Bernard Jardot

Warren Jarvis

Oscar E. Johnson

Robert L. Johnson

Morris Jowett

Duane Kaylor
Maynard Kaylor
Milo Keesler
Forest Keller
Howard Keller
Lewis Keller
James Kelsey
Francis Kidendall
Luman C. Kikendall
Lyle Kinyon
Clayton Kowalk
Robert Lake
George A. Lambert
Kenneth Lambert
Floyd Lambkin
Roy Lampkin
Alfred J. Lane
Slon J. Lane
Duane Lawhead
Wilson Leak
Max LeFever
Harry Leseney
Paul Littlefield
David C. Lloyd
Douglas W. Lloyd
Max Long
Robert J. Long
Rolland Marker
* Glen W. Marr, Jr.
M.J. Martin
Kaye Maupin
Jack J. McFarland
Martin McNamara
Rex Menzer
Richard Merritt
Douglas Merwin
* Delbert S. Meyers
Herbert Milbourn
Allen H. Miller
Claire Miller
Donald L Miller
Frank J. Miller
Homer D. Miller
Paul T. Miller
*Ralph Edward Miller
Robert Miller

Royston Miller
Lynn B. Miller
Clifford Mitchell
Kenneth G. Mock
Murray Moore
Bryce D. Morrill
Gerald Nesse
Albert Newman
William Dale Nicholas
Robert Nickerson
Robert J. Norris
Clinton Palmer
Orville F. Paquette
Frank Parr
Frank Parr, Jr.
Richard Patterson
* Robert S. Peck
Harland Peck
Anthony Petrakovitz
Moxie Petrakovitz
Stanley Phinney
Harold Pitcher
Homer Pollard
T. G. Pollett
Woodrow Pollett
Gordon Poor
Carl Post
Rupert J. Pratt
Richard Price
Anthony Proctor
George E. Punter
Clifford Raymer
Leon A. Raymond
Jimmy Rehfuss
Kenneth Rhines
Robert L. Rhines
Thomas A. Riegel
* Lee W. Robbins
George J. Robinson
Douglas Rockwood
Kenneth Roffman
Arlo H. Rogers
Robert Root
Albert Rose
Wilfred Rouse
Allison Rumrill

Wayne W. Sangree
Alfred C. Schnepp
Dallas Schultz
Harvey Schultz
Jack Schwied
* Paul Scott
Cyril Scott
Howard Scott
Ira Warren Scott
Alden G.Sheets
Sheldon Shepardson
Winfield Shepardson
Floyd Simmons
Paul Simpson
Roy Leon Sims
Harvey D. Slate
Jessie Slentz
Harold Small
Allen Smith
Donald D. Smith
James E. Smith
Neil Smith
Robert C. Smith
Harry Snow
Jerry Snow
Preston Snow
Ray E. Snow
Robert Southwick
Howard Sowle
Richard Spicknell
James Squires
Roy A. Stage
Charles C. Stahl
* Edgar D. Stark
Harold L. Steele
John Steele
William J. Steele
Max Stevens
Keith Stimer
Eugene Stofflet
John Stofflet
Donald A. Strang
Donald Stuart
Walter Sullenbarger
Loren Swanson
George H. Swift

Vincent J. Terczyak
Keith Terrill
Bryce Thomson
Richard Toncray
Frank Towers
Keith Town
Claire Towns
Robert Towns
Harry J. Tracey
Edward E. Tracy
Russell Tripp
Leon C. Troutner
Harley Twichell
Harvey Twichell
John Tyson
Howard Umbarger
Dr. Bert Van Ark
Lewis VanPatten
Rolland VanRiper
Elmer Vantrese
Richard Vincent
Richard Vinson
* Anthony Walters
Lyle Walworth
Victor Walworth
John Weaver
Jack Lamar Webb
Robert Webster
Keith W. Weeks
Robert E. West
Wilber West
L. B. Wheeler
Robert Whipp
Ernest White
Gerald White
Raymond White
Russell White
Irvin Whitehead
Roland Wilbur
Charles H. Williams
Donald Williams
Dawn Wilson
Paul W. Winder
Duane Winright
J. Dean Winter
Robert Winters

Frank D. Wintle

Edward Wolf

Roy Woodman

* Louis Worden

Cecil Wright

Jack Xander

Phil Yerxa

William Young

Bill Zavitz

Richard Zentmyer

Navy

Carson Ackley

Richard G. Allison

Vincent J. Anderson

Robert Babcock

Walter Babcock

Daly Baker

Harold F. Baker

William E. Baker

F. A. Bell

George H. Bellows

Ray Bentley

Paul E. Boatman

Alden J. Bradford

Kyle R. Bradford

Lyle W. Bradford

Dell J. Bramble

Richard F. Bristol

John W. Brumit

Howard Burgess

Russell Burgess

Kenneth Burns

Dale Caarpenter

Lawrence A .Calvin

George S .Canfield

Neil R. Carpenter

Earl Carrier

Maurice Castelein

Albert Challender

Wayne L. Childs

Bill Church

Judson Clapper

Herbert M. Clark

Allen Cook

Milton Cook

Milton M. Cook

D. Crandall
Harold Leon Davis
Richard V. Davis
Leon R. Dean
Dewey Decker
Robert D. DeGeus
Kenneth Charles Degg
Lester Devenney
Leslie DeWaters
Garfield Dowding
Charles Doxtader
Richard Doxtader
Frederick Ebright
Richard L. Eckhart
Richard Burton Ferris
Lyle Wayne French
Raymond G. Fuller
Lawrence A. Galvin
William D. Galvin
Ivan Gillett
Anson D.Grimes
Robert Gulliver
Everett L.Hamilton
Burnell Hansen
Christie W.Hansen
Max Harris
Richard A. Hawley
Keith J. Hayter
George Henry
Robert Higbie
Robert Higdon
Samuel Higgins
Don L. Holgate
Gerald Eugene Holloway
Margaret Holwig
Arthur Hughey
Keith Huntington
Neil Huntington
Dick Jarvix
Murlend Jaycox
Charles H. Keeler
Ronald B. Keller
Clare Keyes
Kenneth L. Kipp
George Klanecky
Van Knowlton

John Krawczyk
D. D. Letts
Donald C. Lockwood
David R. Lonsberry
Clifford Mahan
Leonard Malipsey
Dean W. McConnell
Thomas McCullough
Maurice McKessey
Marvin McKessy
Edwin G. McMullen
John McMullen
George LaVerne Miller
John F. Miller
Spencer Miller
Ralph F. Natusch
Selnor Noble
Barchard Elwin Norton
Dean Odiorne
Edward Page
Robert Palmer
Vernon Parmenter
Richard E. Peacock
Dick Pettit
Hallet E. Pettit
Delbert E. Philo
David Pierce
Glenn B. Ranney
William M. Redfield
Arnold Reed
Clayton R. Robbins
Mark Sackett
Louis Schmidt
A. Charles Schultz
L.W. Scott
George Seelye
Douglas Serrels
Elwin Serrels
Arthur Simpson
K. Simpson
Floyd D. Slate
Louie Smith
Kenneth Spencer
Forrest P. Squires
Robert Squires
Edgar H. Stahl

Max Stofflet

Jack Stoken

Daryl Strickling

Marvin M. Sutton

Wesley Swan

Howard Thompson

James G. Tingley

John G. Tompliff

Mourice Trimble

Kenneth Umbarger

Maurice L. Umbarger

James Robert Watkins

Donald White

George Whitehead

Maurice Whittum

Wayne G. Whittum

Albert D. Wilbur

Nole Wildt

Jack Williams

Robert D. Williams

Robert Wilson

Gleeland H. Winslow

Richard Winters

Ernest Woodman

Murl Woodman

Kenneth Worth

Marines

Claude Bonta

Bernard Bush

Ronald Lee Campbell

Harry Clough

Henry Colestock

Jack Custer

Lyle E. Diehl

Richard H. Finch

Raymond Fisher

Leo E. Gruesbeck

Richard D. Hallifax

William Holwig

Howard K. Horton

Willard Kipp

Richard Miars

Harold Oliver

Glenn E. Olney, Jr.

Harold Sayles

Charlie Sherman

Donald Stanley

William E. Strang

Byron Sweet

Jack William

VernonWilson

Seabees

Kenneth Balcom

Henry Burns

Billy Bush

Clyde Casler

Clarence Conklin

Richard LeRoy Dillingham

Richard Serrels

Wacs & Waves

Leonora Marie Caterino

Eleonor Irene Cheney

Bessie Crandall

Vivian Ellsworth

Gwendolyn Freeman

Betty Heaton

Doris V. Hudson

Bette Milhorn Kennedy

Mary Jane Locke

Isabella Miars-Letts

Helen Riegel

Lois Jo Watkins

Katherine Wheeler

VFW Army

John E. Atkinson

Ray Ball

Joseph C. Ballentine

Harry S. Beaver

Donald Berkman

Bennie P. Carr

Joseph F. Chadwick

Maurice Chadwick

John Colgan

Dwayne DeVeau

William G. Donald

Clarence Donovan

Homer Frazier

Dan Hendrickson

George Hendrickson

Chester Henry

Charles A. John

Charles C. Knowles

Thomas Merrill

Charles C. Miars

Robert Pippin

Clarence Powers

Robert Ray

George B. Seafort

Grant J. Seafort

* Lawrence Sims

Wilbur Stoltz

Ray W. Stone

* Anthony Walter

Edward Winter

VFW Navy & Marines

William Adams

Curtis Allen

Harold Ball

Stanley W. Berkman

Ora Berkman, Jr.

William L. Bever

Cordon Biddle

Warren Biddle

C. Lawrence Bonta

Frank Bonta

Steve Bostick

Tom Bostick

Ferdinand Bowden

Wallace Bowden

Donald Bradish

Robert Bradish

Bill Carr

Oscar Champod

Samuel Dedian

Charles Donnelly

Lewis L. Heaton, Jr

George Hendrickson

Leon H. Hendrickson

Harold Hovey

R. Bruce Kanouse

Richard Tapp Kopel

James T. Miars

Clyde A. Morgan

LaMar Neibaur

Howard T. Powers

Lester E. Ray

Anthony W. Rhodes

Joseph A. Rhodes

Bert Sherman

Lewis Sims

James R. Smith

James Stillwell

John Stoltz

Ira D. Stone

John P. Torrence

B. A. Whitehill

R. B. Willoughboy

Harold Wright

Hershell Max Wright

Merchant Marines

Virginia Berkman

Clifford Alden Bruck

Dana Halsey

Russell K.Winslow

Made in the USA
Lexington, KY
10 February 2010